BY DESIGN

BY DESIGN

God's Distinctive Calling for Women

Susan Hunt

LEGACY COMMUNICATIONS
Franklin, Tennessee

Unless otherwise noted, all Scripture quotations are from the Holy Bible, New
International Version. © 1973, 1978, 1984, International Bible Society. Used
by permission of Zondervan Bible Publishers.

All stories are used by permission. In a few cases, the names have been
changed.

ISBN 1-880692-12-0

Legacy Communications
P.O. Box 680365
Franklin, Tennessee 37068-0365

There is a **Leader's Guide** available for this book
which gives lesson plans for an interactive study of
each chapter, worksheets to be duplicated for
participants, ministry ideas for your women's ministry,
and resources to strengthen the women's ministry in
your church. This Leader's Guide may be ordered by
calling: 1-800-283-1357.

To my grandsons
Hunter and Daniel Barriault

With the prayer
that God will design helpers suitable
for each of you, and with the commitment to
you to do all that I can to teach the women
who are mothering and grandmothering
the little girls you may marry
about the wonder and beauty
of woman's helper design.

CONTENTS

ACKNOWLEDGMENTS

This is not *my* book. So many people have contributed to the ideas, and these ideas have been brewing for so long, that I do not know which ideas belong to whom, and it really doesn't matter since all of us only want to promote Christ and His Kingdom.

Over the last few years I have had conversations with many people that sparked another idea, or sent me in another direction, or clarified a thought. I especially remember a conversation with Paige Benton that brought clarity and crispness to the helper design concept. Another conversation with Lynn Brookside gave insight into some issues that I needed to understand. And countless conversations with Barbara Thompson drove me to dig deeper. Her continual prodding to "exhaust Scripture" holds my feet to the fire.

But no one listened more often or more patiently than my husband Gene. Without his encouragement and endorsement there would be no book.

Dennis Bennett occupies the office across the hall from mine. He read each chapter as it was written. His chapter-by-chapter support kept me going.

Jane Brooks and Stacey UpDeGraff were wonderful as always. Their help in tracking down the "real stories of real women" was persistent and determined. And I am grateful to those real women who were willing for me to share their stories with you. These stories show us what the helper design looks like in real life.

Charles Dunahoo, Diane Langberg, Georgia Settle, Carolyn Lonas, Debbie Trickett, and Patsy Kuiper were wise advisors and contributors for whom I am grateful.

An indispensable contribution was made by women who prayed for this project. I will only fully know in eternity the extent and power of those prayers.

My family prays for me and they protect me from myself. They tell me when it is time for a break, and they provide the fun and games! Our oldest daughter Kathryn always seems to have a baby right in the middle of my most intense projects—that has a delightful way of calling a halt to whatever I'm doing! And the Atlanta Braves have a way of coming back when all seems hopeless and making a mad dash for the championship. That has a way of luring Gene and me to the TV with bowls of frozen yogurt. I would probably explode without these diversions.

And to the wonderful people at Legacy I express my gratitude. George Grant has done more than encourage me to write. He has affected what I write because I read what he writes. George has influenced my thinking and my living, and that influence spills over onto every page I write.

INTRODUCTION

This is my third book. Though each one stands alone, in my mind they form a trilogy. One of the intensities of my life, and the common theme of these books, is to encourage substantive women's ministries in local churches. So whereas each book is hopefully helpful for individual use, I think they are most beneficial when used for group study (a Leader's Guide is available for each book). Together they form a "curriculum package" for developing or strengthening a women's ministry.

Leadership for Women in the Church, co-authored with Peggy Hutcheson, encourages utilizing the full range of the gifts of women without violating male headship in the church. The objective for its use as a group study is to present a vision and suggestions for a relevant women's ministry in the church, and to help women develop leadership skills that will enable them to implement their vision.

Spiritual Mothering is a call to women to return to the Titus 2 model of women mentoring women. The objective for group study is to develop nurturing relationships between women in various seasons and circumstances of life.

The objective of this book is to build upon the first two. Once there is a vision for a vigorous women's ministry, and that ministry is developing nurturing relationships among the women, it is time to equip and mobilize women for ministries of mercy and compassion. We should not try to launch women out into ministry apart from a well-crafted women's ministry that can give training and direction within the context of the Church. Neither should we push women towards ministry apart from secure relationships.

This book has a limited scope. It is not an attempt to do what others have ably done in answering the Biblical feminist, in exegeting Biblical passages that deal with women, or in justifying the Biblical position of male headship.

It is a crusade to present the helper design of women.

It is a challenge to the daughters of Zion to explore our distinctiveness and to return to our Biblical calling.

It is a call to the Church to equip and mobilize its daughters to confront culture with the Biblical truth about womanhood.

And it is a conviction that grace-empowered women can help a hurting world and capture the culture for Christ, one woman at a time.

The helper design was stamped upon woman at creation, and since that time countless women have displayed it beautifully. We will reinforce the implications of our creational design by looking at women in history and contemporary women who have been and are faithful to this calling.

I have been greatly encouraged by a beautiful old book discovered by my friend Georgia Settle in a used bookstore. The name of the author is not given; she is identified as "a daughter of the Schonberg-Cotta family." Neither is the publication date given, but the owner of the book wrote the date 1881 on the title page. The title of the book is *Sketches of The Women of Christendom,* and in the Introduction the author writes:

> I have been asked to bring before you, our Indian sisters, what Christianity has done and can do for women, by telling you stories of the beautiful lives of Christian women from the days when Christ our Lord was born of a woman, to our own. I shall delight to try to do this. . . . As I wonder how best to introduce the subject to you, a beautiful and blessed company seems to rise before me. . . . They shine on us for a time, in some deed of sacrifice and service, and then they are lost to sight again, hidden in the homes they bless.

> They do not wish to be seen, although, if necessary, they do not fear to be seen. The deepest influence of women flows silently, like a quiet stream hidden among the leaves and blossoms it keeps green. . . . Christianity has exalted the ideal of womanhood, not by chang-

ing it, but by showing that the true life of woman, which is love, is
the very essential Being of God; for it is written that "God is love."

In two ways, chiefly, the lives of good and great women are illu-
mined for us through the mists of time, so as to be visible afar off.

Either the natural world of woman, which is the home, is lifted up to
our sight by lofty rank, or is laid bare by especial sorrows, so that
the beauty of the lives lived there, as in countless unknown homes
beside them, is shown openly to the world.

Or, the natural gifts of womanhood are, by especial natural circumstances, or by an overmastering passion of pity, poured forth to
remedy the sorrows and combat the sins of the wide world outside
the home.

Thus two beautiful companies of good women rise radiant before
us: firstly, that of the daughter, the wife, the mother, the sister,
treading the common path of duty, but brought into the vision of the
world by some especial blaze of glory, or some peculiar fires of
sorrow. And then the glorious army of succor: matrons and maidens,
old and young, rich and poor, pouring out the treasures of woman's
heart to relieve the sick, the suffering, the sinful, throughout the
world . . . a great multitude whom no man can number, ceaselessly
shedding benedictions on the world.[1]

The charm of these words is only surpassed by their truth.
Many of the stories told by this daughter of Zion to the women in
India are sprinkled throughout this book. The historical and contemporary stories of women who have brilliantly displayed their
helper design have caused my spirit to soar. I pray that you will
also be stimulated to ascend the heights of our helper design.

Part I

DAUGHTERS OF ZION

In the Old Testament, Zion refers to the fortified mound between the Kidron and Tyropean valleys. When David captured this area, it became known as the city of David. It sometimes refers to the temple vicinity and even to Jerusalem itself. Sometimes it includes the entire nation.

> *Walk about Zion, go around her,*
> *count her towers,*
> *consider well her ramparts,*
> *view her citadels,*
> *that you may tell of them to the next generation.*
> *For this God is our God for ever and ever;*
> *he will be our guide even to the end.*
> *(Psalm 48:12-14)*

This imagery is so rich! And when we realize that in the new covenant, Zion has reference to the Church, it becomes intensely personal and current. Part 1 searches out the privileges and responsibilities of being a daughter of Zion.

> *Say to the Daughter of Zion,*
> *"See, your Savior comes!*
> *See, his reward is with him,*
> *and his recompense accompanies him."*
> *(Isaiah 62:11)*

WENDELMUTA KLAUS

When Martin Luther nailed his ninety-five theses to the church door in Wittenburg, Germany, in 1517, the spiritual darkness that had hovered over the world was punctured. The next few years were turbulent as the light of Biblical truth penetrated that darkness with greater and greater intensity.

The darkness resisted, but truth persisted:

The core of the whole movement was the conflict between the Word of God and the powers of darkness that could not abide it. In each country of Europe the starting-point of the Reformation was the release of the Bible from a dead language to its own language, and the outpouring of the Holy Spirit on those who read and received the wonderful message of free salvation.

The Reformation produced many heroes and heroines of faith:

Each had an individual role to play that helped the Reformation forward, but at the cost of suffering, and in some cases even martyrdom. It was not loyalty to a set of new ideas that sustained them, but the grace of the Lord Christ whom they loved and who made each a useful instrument for His work.

In the Netherlands, Charles V imposed severe penalties on anyone who possessed a Bible or Reformed writings, preached Reformed doctrines, harbored such preachers, or attended their meetings. Hundreds were beheaded, burned, or drowned for refusing to comply with these laws. Wendelmuta Klaus, a widow and known Protestant from Monickendam in North Holland, was apprehended in 1527. She was examined before the Stadholder of Holland, Count van Hoogst, and a great council.

When told that unless she renounced her errors a dreadful death awaited her, she replied:

"If the power is given you from above, I am prepared to suffer."

"You do not fear death because you have never tasted it," they said.

"True, neither shall I taste it, for Christ has said, 'If any man keep my sayings he shall never see death.'"

After a series of questions, she was asked, "Who has taught you these opinions and how have you come by them?"

She replied, "The Lord who calls all men to Him: I am one of His sheep, therefore I hear His voice."

Many more questions were put to her, all of which she answered readily with Scripture quotations. Her examiners were enraged at her calmness and sent her back to prison. She was visited by monks, priests, women, and even relatives, all exhorting her to give in to the higher authority. One noble lady visiting her said, "Dear mother, can you not think as you please and be silent? Why should you die?"

"Ah!" she answered, "You know not what you say. It is written, 'With the heart we believe to righteousness, with the tongue we confess to salvation.' I cannot be silent, dear sister, I cannot be silent. I am commanded and constrained to speak out by Him who has said, 'Whosoever shall confess me before men, him will I confess before my Father which is in heaven. But whosoever shall deny me before men him will I also deny before my Father which is in heaven.'"

"I am afraid," said the lady, "that they will put you to death."

"If tomorrow they burn me or put me in a sack and drown me, to me it is a matter of indifference," said Wendelmuta. "If such be the Lord's appointment it must come to pass; not otherwise. It is my purpose to cleave to the Lord."

She was brought the next day before the council . . . and after another short examination was condemned to death. . . . From the council hall she was led out to a scaffold, strangled, and then burnt.[1]

"I cannot be silent, dear sister, I cannot be silent." And the words of Wendelmuta Klaus continue to be heard.

≥≥   ≥≥   ≥≥

Chapter 1

DISTINCTIVENESS

"For Zion's sake I will not keep silent, for Jerusalem's sake I will not remain quiet, till her righteousness shines out like the dawn, her salvation like a blazing torch."
(Isaiah 62:1)

The crux of this book is my commitment to two profound truths:

Men and women are different.

It's okay that men and women are different.

Male-female distinctiveness is profound because this is a spiritual truth. Since spiritual truth must be "spiritually discerned" (I Corinthians 2:14), these are realities that can only be fully comprehended, appreciated, and lived out by Christians who hold to the authority of God's Word and who are empowered by the Spirit of Truth. Thus it seems to me that we have a profound responsibility to do that which God has enabled us to understand.

The passion of this book is my delight in our feminine design, my dismay that the feminist agenda is robbing us of our distinctiveness as women, and my deep desire for Christian women to honor our Creator by experiencing and exemplifying the beauty of His design.

Male-female distinctiveness is a passionate issue because human sexuality runs deep in our souls. We long to know our person and our purpose. Our identity is gender-specific. The fact that "God created man in his own image, in the image of God he created him, male and female he created them" (Genesis 1:27) resonates into every fiber of our being.

We are living in what some call the decade of women. I find this an interesting notion. I'm not sure what it means, but I have a strong suspicion that those who are making this claim have a definite agenda. It seems to me that those who are setting this agenda are the militant feminists, and one of the items highest on their agenda is that role distinctions must be abolished. Their voices are getting louder and louder. And quite frankly I am simply not willing to sit back and let theirs be the only female voice being heard.

"For Zion's sake I will not keep silent, for Jerusalem's sake I will not remain quiet." (Isaiah 62:1).

Zion and Jerusalem have a much broader meaning than the geographical places. They refer to the City of God, the covenant community, the Church. It is for the sake of the Church that we must not keep silent. I am aware of the Scriptures that talk about women having a quiet and gentle spirit, but they are talking about a woman's relationship with her husband. I am talking about our relationship with culture, and there are times when Christian women must stand and speak against unbiblical cultural trends.

This is one of those times.

If men are the only ones speaking to this issue, non-Christian women will label them as sexist and ignore their call to righteousness. This is a time and a topic when women must be heard.

The early part of this century was apparently also one of those times. In 1901 William Bell Riley, "possibly the most important fundamentalist minister of his generation,"[2] preached a sermon entitled "Woman's Rights and Political Righteousness," in which he stated:

> I recall the first time I ever heard Frances Willard speak. She was in a small southern city, where it was regarded a shame for a woman to appear on the platform with men in the assembly. But I confess, that I went from that house convinced that so long as saloons remained to imbrute women's husbands; blight women's beautiful boys; blast women's lives; and even blacken women's souls, that every speech against it would be justified, no matter who made up their assemblies, and would be approved and applauded by that heavenly assembly of saints and angels . . . when in defense of all that is true, a

suffering woman feels compelled to break the silence and speak against sin. [3]

Biblical womanhood is at risk. That is bad enough, but if the secularists succeed in taking out Biblical womanhood, the family will go with it. The family as God designed it is dangerously rare today.

The Church must boldly and courageously reaffirm the Biblical truth of our feminine calling. This is not a time for timidity and caution. Women are being swallowed up in the feminist flood. We must rescue them. When we rescue women, we rescue families. When we rescue families, we rescue our culture. There are multitudes of deeply wounded women and deeply deceived women. Their hope is not in political systems, nor in the power of position, nor in the power of psychology. Their only real hope is in the Gospel of Jesus Christ.

The Church must present women with Biblical truth. We must help them develop a Biblical world view that includes a Biblical view of womanhood. We must equip them to confront culture and not be consumed by culture, to transform rather than be conformed to culture. Culture is transformed when the people who make up the culture are transformed. People are transformed by embracing and obeying the truth of the Gospel of Jesus Christ:

> Do not conform any longer to the pattern of this world, but be transformed by the renewing of your mind. (Romans 12:2)

> And we, who with unveiled faces all reflect the Lord's glory, are being transformed into his likeness, with ever-increasing glory, which comes from the Lord, who is the Spirit. (II Corinthians 3:18)

I grieve over the confusion in the souls of women today about their sexuality. I am increasingly convinced that much of the confusion and chaos of our culture is because women have conformed to the pattern of this world and are reflecting the world's shame rather than God's glory. And the consequences are horrendous.

Confusion among non-Christian women is to be expected. It is the confusion of Christian women that grieves me. God's calling does not demean His daughters. Biblical womanhood is a high calling that gives confidence and significance to women. Yet it seems that women are floundering in confusion about who they are in Christ and about the application of their faith into their lives.

College women ask, "What are my options as a Christian? Who are my models? Is it wrong to want to succeed in my profession?"

Single women ask, "Do I have to get married before I am complete?"

Wives ask, "What does submission really mean for women today?

Mothers ask, "Is it wrong for a Christian woman to work outside the home?"

Empty-nesters ask, "What do I do now that the children are grown?"

Widows ask, "Where do I find my identity now?"

They all ask, "What is my role in the Church? Is there a place for me?"

There is much that could be said about Biblical womanhood, but one basic, foundational truth is found in God's creation of woman. I believe this truth will give women the security and the conviction they need to confront our cultural confusion with clarity and integrity. When God created man, He said:

"It is not good for the man to be alone. I will make a helper suitable for him" (Genesis 2:18).

HELPER DESIGN

Men-bashing is popular among some today. You've heard the jokes: When God created man He said, "I can do better than that," so He made a woman. That's not right. God did just fine when He made men. He made exactly what He intended to make.

He did not say that man was not good; He said that it was not good for the man to be alone. The presence of a helper was necessary before God gave the pronouncement, "It is very good."

Is it too much of a stretch to think the same is true today? Surely the presence of woman is as necessary to give completeness to the home, Church, and society as was Eve's presence in the garden. It was Adam's aloneness that was not good. The garden would not have been good if women had been alone. God's design is male and female. We are different, and our differences are designed to give completeness to our relationships and to our ministries in the Kingdom.

The problem comes when we assign degrees of value to those differences, because this sets the stage for competition. Competition flies in the face of everything God tells us about relating to one another and about serving together. We were created to help, not hinder. We were created to complete, not compete. Competition destroys relationships, and the writer of Proverbs said: "The wise woman builds her house, but with her own hands the foolish one tears hers down" (Proverbs 14:1).

Male headship in the home and Church is Scriptural. But this does not mean that men and women are not equal. The pattern for role differentiation is seen in the Trinity. The Father, Son, and Holy Spirit have different functions, but are equal in substance and power. Male headship does not mean that women are inferior, just as different roles in the Godhead do not mean that there are various ranks. Male headship is not intended to restrain women. Biblical male headship frees women to reflect the reality of our creation.

I don't play chess, but a friend gave me the instructions from The Kids' Book of Chess and said, "I think you will be interested in this." The book explains that the various pieces on the chessboard represent a cross section of medieval life. My friend was right. I found four of the pieces especially intriguing:

> The Castle is the fort, the refuge, the home . . . the Bishop represents the Church. The Church was very much a part of everyone's life in medieval times. When we learn how the pieces move we will find how well the Bishop and the Castle work together. Church and home—a strong combination! . . . The Queen . . . is the only woman on the board, and the most powerful piece. . . . Her moves combine

both that of the home (Castle) and Church (Bishop). Woman, home, and Church—the most powerful combination on the board! . . . the King . . . the unquestioned authority . . . is the most important—but not the most powerful—piece on the board.[4]

Power is not only derived from positions of authority. The power of influence is staggering. Women do not have to fight to gain power. We have it if we will just do what we were designed to do. The people in medieval culture understood this. Why have we lost it? Could it be because we have simply traded our Divine design for something inferior? As one woman said: "What you are saying is so simple that it is radical."

Let me qualify the kind of power I am talking about. This is not personal power for personal gain. This is the power of grace that is "made perfect in weakness" (II Corinthians 12:9). This is the power of being a channel for that grace to influence others for righteousness. This is the strength that is poured into helping others become all they can be for the glory of the King of kings.

The helper design was not and is not a lesser design or an inferior assignment. It does not mean that woman is less capable. Woman's helper design is not so much what we do but rather who we are. It is not the only aspect of who we are, but it is an essential part of our essence.

Our design should not be confused with our position in Christ. Our position is identical to man's position: "There is neither Jew nor Greek, slave nor free, male nor female, for you are all one in Christ Jesus" (Galatians 3:28).

Neither should our design be confused with our various roles. Our roles change: Daughter, student, wife, friend, employee, employer, mother, etc. Our helper design places its stamp upon each role. This design is integrated into all of the various roles a woman may have at any given time. Often those roles will overlap a man's role, or function. In other words, in many situations men and women may do much the same thing. But our design equips us to bring a unique perspective to that role. We put our own female spin on the particular task, and that is as it should be. Our helper design is intrinsic to who we are as women.

The Hebrew word for helper used in Genesis 2:18 is *ezer*. Tracing this word through the Old Testament is fascinating. Most of the time that this word is used, it refers to God.

James Hurley, in his excellent book *Man and Woman in Biblical Perspective,* says: "Some have suggested that the fact that the woman was made to be man's helper, to be a 'helper appropriate to him' . . . indicates that she was intended to be subordinate. This interpretation rests upon a misapprehension of the meaning of 'helper' ('zr). In English, the term can mean 'junior assistant.' It is highly questionable whether this is a legitimate reading of the Hebrew. The term is used to describe one who lends a hand or helps out, frequently in a context of need. It is most often used of God in relation to Israel. Woman's role as 'appropriate helper,' therefore, does not carry with it an implication of subordination. She is the needed helper whom God supplies to end man's loneliness and to work alongside him, not the junior assistant." [5]

When we consider how God is our helper, we can begin to understand the depth and the power of our female design:

> The Lord is seen as the helper of the underprivileged: the poor (Ps. 72:12) and the fatherless (Ps. 10:14; cf. Job 29:12). The psalmist confesses that he has no help but God (Ps. 22:11; 107:12). He is conscious of divine assistance at a time of illness (Ps. 28:7), at a time of oppression by enemies (Ps. 54:4), and at a time of great personal distress (Ps. 86:17). God's hand (Ps. 119:173) and his laws (Ps. 119:175) were sources of assistance to the psalmist.[6]

As we explore these verses in the second part of this book, we will see that the helper qualities are consistent with our femaleness. Our nurturing, relational strengths grow out of our helper design. The helper verses have exciting implications in showing how women bring completeness to relationships and to ministries.

If women even scratch the surface of the meaning of our calling, we will not listen to the voices that tell us that equality means sameness. This message denigrates womanhood; Scripture validates womanhood.

We must not dilute the worth of our design as women by capitulating to the voices in our culture that say we have to do the same things as men in order to have value. We must be pro-active in declaring the Biblical agenda for womanhood to our culture.

LIFE-PURPOSE

But to capture culture for King Jesus, we must first be captivated by Jesus. We must have a consuming passion for the glory of the Triune God.

So the core question is not what is my role, but what is my goal? What is my chief end?

It is essential to recognize that I am created in the image of God for the purpose of reflecting His image. Sin marred that image, but through the life, death, and resurrection of Jesus Christ that image can be restored. Sovereign grace regenerates me so that I can believe and empowers me so that I can reflect the image of God—regardless of gender. As a person I am called to glorify the Lord God. But I cannot, and should not try to, escape the fact that I am a female and that I am to glorify God as a female person.

If my life-purpose is God's glory, then I will value and affirm male and female differences because I know those differences were designed by God to bring completeness to the relationships He gives me and to the ministries He equipped me to perform.

Christian men and women have an opportunity to proclaim to the world that role differentiation is Biblical and that it is enjoyable. But we must operate on the foundation of sound theology. Sound theology is God-centered and not self-centered; it rests solidly on sovereign grace. Any discussion of male and female distinctiveness can quickly become a self-centered pursuit unless we are focused on the glory of our Sovereign God. Sound theology can help us maintain this focus even as we explore the issue of our distinctiveness as women.

This means that we must examine our hearts. Is our objective women's rights? Are we fighting to get what we "deserve"? Or is our objective God's glory? Are we honestly seeking the honor of our God? These questions put us in the uncomfortable position of searching our hearts to know our motives. As we pursue this path, let us continually pray that God will shine the searchlight of His Word into our hearts and cleanse us from self-interest. Let us ask Him to "create in me a pure heart, O God, and renew a steadfast spirit within me" (Psalm 51:10).

A pure heart and a steadfast spirit will give us the character and the courage to sound a clarion call to women to return to our calling. It is time for women of Biblical faith to reclaim our territory. We know the Designer. We have His instruction manual. If we don't display the Divine design of His female creation, no one will. But if we do, it will be a profound testimony to a watching, needy world.

Male-female distinctiveness is not just an abstract concept that has little to do with the way we go about living our lives. This is a basic ingredient of our world view that determines how we confront our culture. Sally White understands this.

A HELPER MODEL

I met Sally after speaking to a gathering of women from the McLean Presbyterian Church in McLean, Virginia. She is a single, professional woman and serves on her church's women's ministry team, which assists those who are grieving. When she introduced herself, I was struck by her gentle beauty and quiet demeanor. I also had the feeling that I had seen her before. "Thank you for what you said about womanhood," she said. "I have been in a situation with militant feminists for the last few months. What you said was not only refreshing for me—it was therapeutic."

When I questioned Sally, she explained that she had been appointed by President Bush to serve on the commission to study women serving in combat. They had recently released their report, which, briefly stated, would keep women from combat duty on the ground or in aircraft, but permit them on combatant ships.

Then I remembered where I had seen her. "Did I see you last week on the morning news?" I asked.

Sally, a Master Sergeant in the Air Force Reserve, had defended the commission's report on numerous national television news programs. As I watched her being interviewed on the "Today" program, I thought, "She must be a Christian to have her head screwed on so straight about womanhood." Now I found myself talking to the woman I had cheered for as she was harassed by the woman taking the opposite position in the interview. I was not surprised to find out that she was a Christian, but I was surprised at her shyness. I realized that being pushed into the spotlight was not something Sally White desired nor, in her words, "had ever remotely imagined. I calmed myself in these situations by telling myself that the Lord put me on this committee and that I should be thankful for the opportunity. This always changed my attitude from one of fear to gratitude," she said.

Several months later, when Secretary of Defense Les Aspin issued a directive instructing the Air Force to allow women in combat duty in aircraft, Sally was again called upon for live interviews. When I watched her calm and clear statements, I knew that her boldness did not come from a "natural" tendency. I knew I was watching the supernatural results of a covering of prayer. Whenever Sally was interviewed, the prayer chain of her church was activated. Her response to one interviewer who asked her reaction to the directive shows her character and her courage:

> I believe this is a sad day when our nation's leaders will unnecessarily put women into harm's way where women will be killed, where they will be expected to kill. This isn't progress. This is not elevation of women. It is a tragic loss of civility for our nation and loss of respect for our women. This change is being done solely for purposes of political expediency and it is not based on logic, it is not based on truth, nor on military necessity. The Clinton administration has just thumbed their nose at a report which cost the taxpayers four million dollars and which found overwhelming evidence that it is not in the best interest of our nation to put women into combat roles.

The decision of the political powers went to the feminists, but theirs was not the only female voice that was heard. For Zion's sake, Sally White refused to be silent. Thanks, Sally!

As we focus on the distinctiveness of our female design, I pray that the imaginations of the daughters of Zion will pulsate with the implications of our calling. And I pray that you will share my passion to display the female design fashioned by the Master Designer at the creation of His world.

But first we must consider the distortions of woman's creation design. Understanding the distortions will help us avoid being confused or deceived by them.

SARAH MARTIN

Sarah Martin was an unlikely activist. She was an orphan who barely eked out a living for herself and her aged grandmother by working as a seamstress. Six days a week she labored, but on the Sabbath she taught in a Sunday School for poor children:

> Often on her way to her work, or to the school, this young dressmaker happened to pass the jail or common prison of the town. Her heart yearned with pity to the degraded criminals shut up in it. No effort had yet been made to reclaim them. No good men or women visited them. It was like a refuse-heap of humanity, avoided by all. . . . Sarah Martin yearned to rekindle the dying embers of the divine fire in the hearts of these most forsaken and degraded of our Lord's redeemed creatures.

> For years this compassionate yearning rose and grew in her heart, silently organizing itself into an imperishable purpose, strengthened by prayer to God, and never weakened by idle prattling about it to others.

Sarah's compassion was activated when a mother was thrown into prison for beating her own child:

> She asked permission to go and see the poor, abandoned creature. . . . She made her first step into that closed den of misery and iniquity. . . . She spoke to the miserable, cruel woman of her own guilt, and of the infinite pity of God. The poor creature, who thought that God and man were against her, as she had been against all that is most sacred to man and to God, burst into tears at these faithful words of loving rebuke, and listened, a broken-hearted penitent, as the sisterly lips repeated to her the words uttered so long ago as they were nailing the Holy Jesus on the cross—"Father, forgive them; for they know not what they do."

> That was the first step in Sarah Martin's five and twenty years of patient labor.

By degrees she was admitted regularly into the prison, and by degrees she devoted more and more of her time to the work of rescue, sacrificing two of her working days to the prisoners, and living contentedly on the diminished earnings of the rest.

She succeeded in touching the conscience and winning the trust of the most hardened men and women; and, what is almost harder, she succeeded in inspiring the love of labor into the most lazy, conquering the helpless indolence which is the source of so much moral malaria and disease . . . she awakened many of them to see, through her life and words, the Savior who was the source of the pity in her heart, who would go with them into the world of temptation beyond the prison.

She was most ingenious, in her poverty, in turning everything to good account for her prisoners; straw for them to plait hats with, bits of cloth for patchwork, bones to make knives and spoons, scraps of paper or pasteboard, leaves of worn-out, torn old books. She had wonderful skill in discovering or waking up their especial tastes and faculties, sometimes, for instance, giving them good drawings to copy, and so opening a new world of interest to any who had artistic gifts.

She did not forsake her poor pupils when they left the prison for the world. . . . She did everything she possibly could to set them going again in the right way, ingeniously varying her methods according to their needs and characters, as a wise mother would for her own children.

For one she bought a donkey, to carry loads of fish from the fishermen on the coast to the inland villages; for another, scales, and a little store of fish to sell; for another she would intercede with a former master.

In all, she tried to awaken again the life of home affections and duties; for all she labored, to guard them against their former evil companions; for the poor girls she established an evening school to keep them from temptation. And we must not forget that these labors of love were carried on by one herself poor, and by no means above the danger of want.

In a little book which she wrote, she tells us her secret: "My mind, in the contemplation of such trials, seemed exalted by more than human energy; for I had counted the cost, and my mind was made up. If, while imparting truth to others, I became exposed to temporal want, this privation, so momentary to an individual, would not admit of a comparison with following the Lord, and thus administering to others."

And so the beautiful life went on to the end.

She was not suffered to want; though the provision came to her as to the birds of heaven, in daily handfuls, and not in overflowing barns.

She was not, indeed, exempted from suffering, in her last illness. . . . About twenty minutes before her death, this lowly and faithful disciple, in her great anguish, asked for an anodyne to still the pain.

Instead of giving it her, and so dulling her last conscious moments here, the nurse told her her hour was come.

"Thank God! Thank God!" she said, and pressed and clapped her feeble hands together in token of victory.

And so she died, and went among the blessed and great multitude of those who have overcome.[1]

It was neither political expediency nor personal gain that caused Sarah Martin's activism. She was driven by a passion for the Savior. Her prison ministry was simply an expression of her love for Him. When she visited them in prison, she visited Him in prison (Matthew 25: 34–40).

ða   ða   ða

Chapter 2

DISTORTIONS

"We look for light, but all is darkness; for brightness, but we walk in deep shadows. Like the blind we grope along the wall, feeling our way like men without eyes . . . truth has stumbled in the streets, honesty cannot enter. Truth is nowhere to be found, and whoever shuns evil becomes a prey."
(Isaiah 59:9, 10, 14, 15)

$\mathbf{A}$s we race toward the twenty-first century, we are in a cultural crisis. This is a defining moment in our culture. We no longer live in a nation where there is a Christian consensus. We live, as Francis Schaeffer said, in a post-Christian era. There is a long list of critical issues, but one issue that surely is on the short list is our understanding of gender roles. Human sexuality penetrates the depths of our souls. When we are bewildered about our sexuality, the confusion is unbridled.

Since the fall of Adam and Eve into sin there has been confusion about male-female roles. Sin confuses because it blinds us to truth. But this confusion has been amplified in our day by two distortions: radical feminism and oppressive subjection.

RADICAL FEMINISM

The feminist movement is one part of the larger movement of relativism. The foundational question of our culture is the issue of truth. Is truth relative or is it absolute? The relativist denies that there is such a thing as absolute truth, which is a self-contradiction, because he wants his statement to be believed as absolute truth!

This relativist approach of "whatever is meaningful to me, whatever makes me happy, is truth for me," is totally self-centered and leads to chaos. It is impossible for the unregenerate mind to accept absolute truth because this is a "spiritual truth that must be spiritually discerned" (I Corinthians 2:14). So the unsaved mind concocts all sorts of explanations about life. But these explanations leave people in deep shadows, groping along the wall.

What is interesting about relativism is that one of the most influential forces that has propelled it forward is the feminist segment of the movement. This should not surprise us.

Soon after the creation event, the enemy of truth approached the woman with a lie and she was deceived. Some speculate that he went to her because she was weaker and more vulnerable. I think not. Of course, it is speculation, since Scripture does not give a definitive reason, but I do not believe God's Divine design was weak and vulnerable. She was a helper with incredible influence upon her husband. When she willfully yielded to the tempter's lie, and then offered the forbidden fruit to her husband, he did not even whimper a protest. He was not deceived; he was influenced. His helper became his hinderer.

Is it not possible that Satan went to Eve because he knew the power of her influence? Is it not also possible that the lie of relativism has been dangled before women today because the enemy knows that if women bite, the rest will be easy?

Feminism has been a tool to distort truth. It has enticed women with the same bait that hooked Eve—self-promotion rather than God's glory.

Any discussion of the feminist movement should acknowledge that the early traditional women's movement "started with some noble goals: The right to vote, equal opportunities for education, equal pay for equal work, etc. During the framing of the Constitution, Abigail Adams wrote to her husband, John Quincy Adams, urging him to consider the rights of women in wording the Bill of Rights. Her suggestion was not taken seriously, in fact she was laughed at. Perhaps this attitude of not taking women seriously has contributed to the extremes to which the movement has progressed in this century."[2]

Peter Jones, in his book *The Gnostic Empire Strikes Back,* explains another contributing factor and the ominous forecast:

> Radical feminism is, in some sense, an inevitable reaction to and extension of the sexual revolution of the sixties. Unleashed in a culture traditionally patterned on Judeo-Christian ethics, this "liberalization" at first catered to heterosexual male appetites and produced the image of the woman as sexual object. In its own way, this heterosexual revolution was an assault against the image of God in men and women. But now the pendulum has swung in the other direction. Feminism is demanding revenge. Such a movement gets rid of certain expressions of unjustifiable male oppression, but its real ideological goal is to efface any recollection of creational structures. It is surprising that a non-Christian (at least he lays no claim to being a Christian in his books), once feminist thinker, George Gilder, has (since 1973) recognized this ideological agenda whereas the thinking of so many Christians appears naively oblivious. Gilder notes: "The revolutionary members of the women's movement . . . say that our sexual relationships are fundamental to all our other institutions and activities. If one could profoundly change the relations between the sexes, they contend, one could radically and unrecognizably transform the society." Guilder rightly affirms that "sexuality is not simply a matter of Games People Play; it is one of the few matters truly of life and death to society." Thus he warns that if the feminist agenda, even its more moderate version, is carried through, "our society is doomed to years of demoralization and anarchy, possibly ending in a police state."[3]

Jones goes on to warn: "It would be easy to dismiss Guilder as an extremist, but one only has to read in the New Age literature to see that police states are definitely on the final agenda. . . . Certainly we should do all we can to hear Scripture afresh as it pertains to the role and ministry of Christian women. But the specter of the destruction of our God-given sexually differentiated identities in the name of Christ should fill us with righteous loathing and dread."[4]

The ideas of the modern feminist movement were first set forth in the sixties with the publication of Betty Friedan's book, *The Feminine Mystique.* In *The Feminist Gospel* Mary Kassian traces the development of the movement. She explains that it evolved from an attempt to deny gender differences, then to a pride in female differences that led to the belief that female is better, and then to the

> third phase of the development of feminist theory—the spiritual quest. Feminists had progressed from viewing their differences with pride and confidence, to viewing them as deistic in essence. This third phase, which emerged in the late 1970's and early 1980's, focused on esoteric metaphysics—an inner journey of self-discovery that supposedly provided the mystical answer to life's meaning by allowing the seeker to experience connectedness with the universe and with the reality of her own power . . . feminism had convinced women that their own experience was the only valid source of meaning. As this philosophy developed, feminists naturally looked within to discover the "truth" about God. Since they had rejected an external "male god," they sought a new symbol that would affirm the legitimacy of their personal experience and self-definition: the goddess . . . goddess worship was not worship of an external deity; it was, in essence, worship of oneself. The goddess was merely a symbol that acknowledged the legitimacy of self-worship.[5]

Kassian concludes:

> Feminism is, to the evangelical church, a watershed issue. In order to introduce feminist concepts into Christianity, basic beliefs regarding the inspiration and authority of Scripture need to be adjusted. . . . Accepting the feminist precept into one's worldview immediately initiates a change in one's view of truth and absolutes. It places an individual upon a slippery slope which can lead, and usually does lead, far away from God. My point is not that every individual who calls her or himself a feminist is damned to Hell. I am not implying guilt by association. What I am saying is that the presupposition of feminism is not in harmony with the Bible. Accepting the feminist precept, even to a small degree, necessitates some degree of compromise.[6]

The feminist movement today includes women with a wide range of expectations, goals, values, and philosophies. . . . The more radical and vocal group would see anything that advances women in the world as good — even though it is untrue or unlawful. They would rewrite the law and redefine the truth . . . the feminists have redefined the oppression of women to include childbirth, motherhood, home making and anything they think limits a woman's "right" to do and be anything she wishes. They seem to reject any limitation except their own personal, selfish desires. Hence their passionate demand for abortion as a woman's right and lesbianism as an approved lifestyle.[7]

Ron Rhodes gives some helpful definitions of the various "subgroups" of the feminist movement in his article "The Debate Over Feminist Theology." He explains: "These subgroups should not be viewed as having clearly defined lines of demarcation; rather, they are more like clusters along the theological-philosophical continuum. Along this continuum, it is possible that a feminist may fall between the clusters, thereby sharing some of the characteristics of two different groups."[8] He then defines the groups as follows:

Secular feminists are humanists who disallow God, revelation, and religion in the discussion of feminism. They view the Bible as a major source of chauvinist ideas and a relic of antiquity that has no relevance to the ongoing debate over the roles of men and women in modern society.

New Age feminists are pagans who are typically involved in the worship of a feminine deity or goddess.

Liberal Christian feminists operate within a Christian framework but approach feminism (and theology in general) from a very liberal perspective. They believe the Bible writers were simply men of their times and were limited in their perspectives. Liberal Christian feminists employ a "hermeneutic of suspicion"—that is, they systematically assume that the Bible's male authors and interpreters deliberately covered up the role of women in early Christianity. Using such a hermeneutic, it is easy to sift out from the Bible anything one finds offensive to one's feminist tastes.

Evangelical feminists are those who generally (not always) hold to conservative views on the Bible and theology but who nevertheless embrace the feminist ideal of abolishing gender-based roles in society, Church, and home. They believe the Bible is authoritative and, rightly understood, supports their feminist views.[9]

For the militant feminists, males are the enemies and women are the victims. An article in the *U.S. News & World Report* stated:

This is nowhere clearer than in academic feminism. On the campus, in most feminist-studies programs, rape is now the paradigm and central metaphor of male-female relations. What to most of us is a brutal and ugly crime is to conventional feminist academics male business as usual, the image of what men do to women all the time, sexually and non-sexually. In the secular convents of feminist studies, abstruse man-hating and galloping heterophobia are absolutely routine. These attitudes are not much help to real-world women, who have brothers and fathers they love and who might want to get married sometime.[10]

Where has this nonsense taken us?

A frightening illustration was reported by Cal Thomas in his syndicated column.

A Milwaukee attorney made her contribution to last week's "Take Our Daughters to Work Day," orchestrated by the Ms. Foundation, by telling 36 12- and 13-year-old seventh-graders that they should not bother to get married, because marriage can interfere with their careers (and marriages, she said, usually end anyway). The girls would be better off, she suggested, to remain single and "sleep around all you want." The attorney . . . later offered a lukewarm apology: "About that sleeping around thing, you girls are only about 12. Well, that's still very young."[11]

An even more frightening illustration was given to me by my daughter. She told me of seeing a young woman she had not seen in a couple of years. The woman told her that she is now married, "but my husband bores me, so I am having an affair. My mother covers for me because she says that the important thing is whatever makes me happy."

The militant feminists claim to speak for women today. This is not unusual. Generally it is the people at the end of a spectrum who are the most vocal. But the danger of the noise-makers at the end of a spectrum is that their message becomes more palatable as it trickles down the spectrum. We can recognize the absurdity of their radical ideas, but the more we are exposed to their philosophies the more desensitized we become. It seems to me that the trickle down effect of the feminist ideas has come into the Christian community through the "evangelical feminists," who are sending messages to Christian women that I find frightening.

> Their common theme has been the rejection of a unique leadership role for men in marriage and in the Church . . . they differ from secular feminists because they do not reject the Bible's authority or truthfulness, but rather give new interpretations of the Bible to support their claims. . . . What has been the result? Great uncertainty among evangelicals. Men and women simply are not sure what their roles should be. [12]

The issue of male leadership in the Church revolves primarily around the question of authority. Getting bogged down in that controversy is unfortunate, because it sidetracks the Church. It deflects us from presenting the astounding beauty and usefulness of our helper design. This book is not an attempt to justify the position that only men are to be ordained to Church office. I accept that position. My desire is to move beyond that issue and to counteract the distortions by encouraging the Church to embrace and endorse our helper design. I long to see men and women chart a course that will enable the Church to move beyond our own doors and to courageously present Biblical womanhood to our culture.

Whatever form or intensity feminism takes, it is an assault against God's creational design. Any deviation from truth leaves people in deep shadows, groping along the wall.

OPPRESSIVE SUBJECTION

At the other end of the spectrum is a distortion that is quieter and more subtle but still sends a garbled message to Christian women. It is a teaching that substitutes passive subservience for Biblical submission. It is sometimes characterized by a "chain-of-command" model. This is not Biblical submission. When a woman marries, she does not join the military. She does not become a slave. She joins her heart and flesh to a man in a union of love. Biblical submission is an attitude of joyful and willing submission to the God-ordained authority and protection of her husband.

The results of women accepting the feminist agenda are obvious. But we must also admit that there are negative consequences when women accept subjugation. Often when a woman allows herself to be dominated by a man, she suppresses her personality, stifles her spiritual gifts, and suppresses her anger. These women somehow believe that to submit means to become brain dead and passive. But eventually there is a blip on the brain wave, and these women wake up filled with fury. They are angry with men who oppressed them, with themselves for taking it, and often with the Church who taught them that they had no "rights" even when they were mistreated and abused.

Sara is an example. Sara grew up in a Christian family. Her main desire was to please God and to do what is right. She never rebelled, and she matured into a gifted, intelligent, godly young woman. In high school and college she dated only Christian young men. She married her high school sweetheart, who was the pastor's son. What more could parents want for their daughter? How was Sara to know that her marriage to John would be anything less than her dream of two becoming one?

Soon, however, the newlywed couple had friction over the role of a woman. Sara began to notice that the pattern in her husband's family was that of a controlling man and a passive, almost slave-like woman. The man's role was to earn a living, make all decisions in the home, and perform any chores he decided were manly. The woman's role was to raise the children, clean the house, prepare the meals, and to make sure that nothing interfered with the husband's duties. Sara seldom voiced her frustrations, and when she did it was an emotional outburst.

The problems grew when their daughter, Mary, was born. Sara was no longer allowed to work outside the home. At first this was welcomed because she knew the importance of raising children in the nurture and admonition of the Lord. With time, the restraints became more severe. John decided that women's socials and retreats were frivolous wastes of time and money. To go for a walk with a friend or to an exercise class became a battle because John was inconvenienced by watching Mary. For the first time in her life Sara began to rebel inwardly against the person she had loved the most. But she still did not confront the issues, and her anger simmered. Finally she knew they needed help and turned to her pastor for counseling. John consented to go because she had a problem, and the pastor could surely point this out to her. The counseling was unfruitful.

John continues to withdraw from the rest of the congregation and to pour himself into his work. Sara sees the Church as her enemy instead of a safe place to grow and serve her Lord. The marriage has degenerated into two separate people living under the same roof. Their daughter Mary is growing up with this un-Biblical model of marriage and of womanhood.

Male headship does not mean male dominance. Biblical headship does not seek to control or oppress. Submission does not mean passively accepting an unhealthy relationship that is destructive to oneness. Jill Briscoe has said: "Headship means that the man is to make sure the wife's opinion has equal validity with his." Well said!

BIBLICAL SUBMISSION

Submission is a Biblical teaching. Men have been assigned by God to the position of headship in the home and in the Church. In the home, this assignment carries with it the responsibility to "love your wives, just as Christ loved the Church and gave himself up for her . . ." (Ephesians 5:25). And the male leaders in the Church are commanded to "Be shepherds of God's flock that is under your care, serving as overseers—not because you must, but because you are willing, as God wants you to be, not greedy for money, but eager to serve; not lording it over those entrusted to you, but being examples to the flock" (I Peter 5:2-3).

Headship and submission are two sides of one coin. They go together. But neither is exempt if the other forfeits.

Headship and submission begin with a spirit of humility: "Scripture says: 'God opposes the proud but gives grace to the humble.' Submit yourselves, then, to God" (James 4:6-7).

Humility then expresses itself in mutual submission: "Submit to one another out of reverence for Christ" (Ephesians 5:21).

Humility continues to express itself in headship and submission.

Submission, whether it is to God, to one another, to husbands, or to male leadership in the Church, is a grace-empowered virtue of humility and reverence for God. It has nothing to do with superior/inferior status or equality. It has to do with attitude and function. The Father, Son, and Holy Spirit are equal in being and in power, but each has a different function. Whatever our function, we are to carry it out after the pattern of Jesus:

> Do nothing out of selfish ambition or vain conceit, but in humility consider others better than yourselves. Each of you should look not only to your own interests, but also to the interests of others. Your attitude should be the same as that of Christ Jesus:
>
> > Who, being in very nature God,
> >   did not consider equality with God something
> >   to be grasped,
> > but made himself nothing,
> >   taking the very nature of a servant,
> >   being made in human likeness.
> > And being found in appearance as a man,
> >   he humbled himself
> >   and became obedient to death—
> >   even death on a cross!
> >   (Philippians 2:3-8)

We should have the same attitude as Jesus. This means an attitude that does not have to grasp, or seize, what we already have, namely equality before God. It means an attitude that does not have to promote self because we have confidence in God's sovereign design and plan.

Biblical submission cannot be put in a neat little box of specified behaviors or lifestyles. It may be different in different situations and relationships. Essentially, it is a matter of attitude. A woman can express her opinions, be a self-starting high achiever, and still have a submissive attitude. A woman can even "disobey" her husband with a submissive spirit. For example, a woman married to a nonbeliever may have to disobey him in order to obey the Lord. She may have to lovingly say, "I want to be the wife you need me to be, but I cannot go against my conscience and disobey the Lord. I cannot sign my name to a tax form that is not truthful. I would not be helping you to do this."

In the Sara-John illustration above, Sara did not help John by giving in to his oppressive demands. She never should have allowed the problems to ulcerate. They should have been dealt with at the first sign of injury to oneness. However, once separateness has occurred, appropriate action would include fervent prayer for a marriage that reflects Biblical oneness; repentance of anything she had done, was doing, or had failed to do, that damaged oneness; repentance for any blame-shifting she may have done; relinquishment to the Lord of her desires; and then a loving confrontation in a spirit of submission. This confrontation should acknowledge her own contribution to the marriage trauma and should explain her desires and goals for the relationship. The fact that she has relinquished her marriage to the Lord will give her a freedom to accept John's response whether it is negative or positive. Above all, Sara must not withdraw from John, from the Lord, or from His people.

Sometimes women present themselves as super spiritual because they "submit" to their husbands, when in reality they manipulate and control. They are like the little girl who was told by her daddy to sit down in church. She reluctantly obeyed, looked at him with fire in her eyes, and said, "I'm sitting on the outside, but I'm standing up on the inside." That is not Biblical submission!

Headship/submission is Biblical. There is no way around it if we are going to live in obedience to Biblical truth. But there is really no reason to want to get around it unless our agenda is in opposition to God's agenda. His way is the best way. His way frees us to fulfill our creational design. But staying on track requires a constant attitude check. The distortions at each end of the spectrum pull at us. And when women land on either end of the spectrum, the results are just as devastating. When the muscles of our design are not used properly, they atrophy. Some women atrophy into hard, cold, angry people. Some wither into mushy pulp. Neither is appealing! Distortions debilitate emotionally and spiritually.

Biblical truth liberates.

FREE TO BE ME

"If you hold to my teaching, you are really my disciples. Then you will know the truth, and the truth will set you free" (John 8:31-32).

Sally Illman, a pastor's wife from California, discovered this freedom. Here is her story:

Scripture records for us that after Job was cursed he said, "I have no peace, no quietness; I have no rest, but only turmoil" (Job 3:26). Had I been aware of it at the time, that would have been my life verse for most of the 1970s. I was in my 20s, married, and had two children.

The feminist movement was in full swing. Although the Lord protected me from all of the experiences of the movement, I was still influenced by it. I was struggling to find a deeper meaning to my life, to be "me," to find myself. But the searching was all done outside of the context of God, my husband, and my children. The feminists told me that I could be whatever I wanted to be. That was a lie.

With the emphasis on fulfilling me, I ran a gamut of experiences. I read and partially implemented Marabel Morgan's *Total Woman*. That experiment lasted about three days until I exploded from trying to be so sweet under my own strength for my own ends. I read *I'm Okay, You're Okay*, but I had this nagging suspicion that I really wasn't okay. I had been raised in a liberal church, so religion held no solace. I could not understand why God allowed bad things to happen. I had no assurance of a peaceful eternity. A Women's Awareness course was my next try, but that held no answers. I was totally frustrated and afraid that I would never know who I was.

In Psalm 62, David describes a leaning wall, a tottering fence on a lofty place ready to be pushed over. That is the woman who tries to find fulfillment in herself. In contrast to that is what I finally found in the late 1970s. Zephaniah 3:17 says that God "will quiet you with His love." He did that for me. He has shown me that I can find "me" but within the shelter of Him, as a fortress, within His tents, with His hedge around me. He has shown me what I am to be within the context of my husband and my children. I am to use the gifts that God has given me to glorify Him, not me. My priorities are defined as I strive to fulfill myself within the boundaries that God in His loving mercy has given me.

For me, that means that because Bob is a pastor, then I am a pastor's wife. That role is defined for me, but within that role, I can stretch myself to complete fulfillment. We now have four children. How I mother them is an outpouring of my gifts, imagination, and Biblical understanding. What feminists do not understand is that they are much more confined than I. They are limited by time and space. I am only limited by an infinite, all wise God who, as my life progresses, unveils unlimited opportunities that He has for me when He knows that I am ready for them. Instead of striving in frustration to find fulfillment, I am resting in the knowledge that my life has purpose and meaning. Isaiah 32:17 says, "The fruit of righteousness will be peace; the effect of righteousness will be quietness and confidence forever." The feminists have brought frustration and turmoil; the Lord has given us peace.

This daughter of Zion is free to be who she was created to be. That is real freedom!

BALANCE

Biblical truth brings balance into life. My husband is very careful to keep the tires on our car balanced. I asked him why. Knowing that I really did not want the technical answer, he said, "To keep them from wobbling." To wobble means to be insecure, unstable, and weak—to vacillate. Biblical truth keeps us from wobbling. A life balanced by Biblical truth is secure, stable, strong, and unwavering; it reflects harmony and symmetry.

The 90s woman has been ravaged with the ideas of two extremes. But indications are that women are realizing that neither extreme is working. Women are rejecting the absurdity of militant feminism and the oppression of subjection. They are looking for something that does work, something that makes sense.

> We look for light, but all is darkness; for brightness, but we walk in deep shadows. Like the blind we grope along the wall, feeling our way like men without eyes . . . truth has stumbled in the streets, honesty cannot enter. Truth is nowhere to be found. (Isaiah 59)

We have a window of opportunity. Women who are aligned with God's original intent have a waiting audience to view His Divine design. Women want to see a view of womanhood that lines up with reality. God's truth is the ultimate reality.

Women have an awakening desire to discover their design. They are beginning to shun the lie, but "whoever shuns evil becomes a prey. . . ." Women who shun evil are vulnerable. They are helpless and unable to resist attack because they have no weapon. The Church must be there to catch them, to fill in the blanks of their understanding about womanhood, to present truth. But we must not only show them the helper design, we must show them the Designer. Knowing Jesus as the Savior of their souls and the Lord of their lives will empower them to live Biblically as women. He will give them that peace and purpose they seek.

The Church, the defender of truth, must be the defender of Biblical womanhood.

WOMEN
OF THE COVENANT

Women of Christendom have a glorious heritage. For Christian women in America, much of our legacy can be traced back to the time of the Reformation. It was that event that eventually led the Puritans to come to America:

> Our roots also go back to 1662, the year of the Great Ejection, and to the Killing Time of 1660-1668 in Scotland, and the role that women of the Covenant played during those critical years.

> The Great Ejection of 1662 . . . was the time when the preachers were labeled "Puritan" or "non-conformist," when it was known exactly where a man stood theologically and whether he identified with the state church hierarchy or the non-conformists. Those who admitted to being non-conformists were ejected from their parishes—never to return.

> At that time, ministers were paid once annually . . . and all those who were ejected had to flee for their lives to the hills without salary. These Covenanters and their families roamed the hills, without so much as a roof over their heads, depending on brothers and sisters in the Lord for their basic needs to be met. But not even such difficulties as these silenced them. They continued preaching the Word wherever the Lord led them.

The Killing Time referred to a time of great torture against believers by the state church and the national government. People caught praying, or in possession of a Bible, were often shot on the spot. These were dire times for the Covenanters, and there are many heroes and heroines of faith from this period of Church history.

The women were a noble, devoted, and courageous group who walked confidently with the Lord in the midst of great conflicts. Some were martyred. Others felt the bullets of the brutal dragoons (police) on lonely hillsides. They knew the rope of the common hangman on the city scaffold and they knew what it was to be branded on the cheek: a 'C' for a Covenanter or a 'P' for a Puritan. They were tortured, maltreated, and banished from their homes and villages to live in caves, at best, or in huts at worst. Some contracted grave maladies because of their exposure and privation. Many died prematurely. They knew what extreme cruelty meant and what it really cost to take a stand for the Lord Jesus Christ:

There are four women of the Covenant that were outstanding in their love and devotion to "King Jesus." The first was Marion Cameron, a sister of Richard Cameron, well-known Covenanter leader, and her two companions. One day they were discovered on a hillside singing Psalms and sharing Scripture. They were shot on the spot—immediately—because they refused to burn their Bibles.

Two other young women were executed in January of 1681 for attending services at which the powerful Covenanter preacher Donald Cargill was preaching. One of them was Isabelle Allison, who gave a courageous testimony a few moments before her execution. "I lay down my life for owning and adhering to Jesus Christ, he being a free king in his own house, for which I bless the Lord that ever he called me to that."

Of all the women of the covenant Margaret Lauchlison and Margaret Wilson are best remembered. Margaret Lauchlison had many years on her young friend, Margaret Wilson, and had been her principal spiritual mentor. It was their death in the Solway River that is considered to be one of the most terrible acts of the persecution. . . .

The older woman, Margaret Lauchlison, was tied to a stake well out from the beach, and the younger woman, who was only 18 years of age, was fastened to a stake nearer to the shore. As the tidal waters were rising around the older woman and coming close to overwhelming her, the soldiers asked the young girl what she thought of her companion now. She replied, "Ah, what do I see but Christ wrestling there!"

After the water had risen well up around her own body, they drew her to the shore and tried to get her to recant. They offered to save her life if she would only say, "God save the King!" She replied insistently, "God save him if He will, for it is his salvation that I desire." This did not satisfy the men. They again bound her to the stake and watched the waters rising. They called her out again just before she was about to drown. By this time they had her parents, who were not believers, imploring her frantically to turn her back on her faith.

"Will you recant?" the soldiers asked for the last time. "No," she said, "because I love the Lord." And with that she continued reciting Scripture, holding her Bible close to her, repeating the precious Scripture from Romans 8 until the waters totally engulfed her. Young Margaret had already seen the older Margaret praying and reciting Romans 8 to the finish, dying a faithful death for her Lord.[1]

Paul instructed the young preacher Titus to "teach the older women to be reverent in the way they live. . . . Then they can train the younger women . . . so that no one will malign the word of God" (Titus 2: 3–5). The older Margaret was a spectacular example of spiritual mothering. Her obedience to the Titus mandate equipped the younger Margaret to remain faithful to the end.

❧   ❧   ❧

Chapter 3

DEFENDERS OF TRUTH

" . . . the church of the living God,
the pillar and foundation of the truth."
(I Timothy 3:15)

Truth has been distorted. People "walk in deep shadows . . . grope along the wall . . . truth has stumbled in the streets" (Isaiah 59).

Perhaps nowhere is this more obvious than the distortion regarding woman's design. This pillage of womanhood is more than a cultural confrontation. This is a spiritual confrontation that strikes at the very heart of the Creator's creation. This is a battle that is being fought in the heavenlies between light and darkness, between God's truth and Satan's lie. And the defender of truth is the Church of Jesus Christ.

The Church has been designated by God as the "pillar and foundation of truth"(I Timothy 3:15). "The figure is expressive of the fact that the Church is the guardian of the truth, the citadel of the truth, and the defender of the truth over against all the enemies of the Kingdom of God."[2]

By giving His Word to the Church, God constituted the Church the keeper of the precious deposit of the truth. While hostile forces are pitted against it and the power of error is everywhere apparent, the Church must see to it that the truth does not perish from the earth, that the inspired volume in which it is embodied be kept pure and unmutilated, in order that its purpose may not be defeated, and that it be handed on faithfully from generation to generation. It has the great and responsible task of maintaining and defending the truth against all the forces of unbelief and error.[3]

The guardian, citadel, and defender of truth . . . the keeper of the precious deposit of the truth . . .—what beautiful and comprehensive language. A fundamental mark of the Church is faithfulness to God's Word. A presupposition of this book is that any reference to the Church is a reference to those churches which hold to the inerrancy of God's Word and that affirm with the Psalmist, "All your words are true; all your righteous laws are eternal" (Psalm 119:160).

THE CHURCH MILITANT

The Church was never intended to be passive. The Church is to be militant in its defense of truth and righteousness. And we can do so with great confidence because Jesus said," . . . on this rock I will build my church, and the gates of Hades will not overcome it" (Matthew 16:18). The Greek word translated overcome (*katischuo*) means to overpower, to prevail. This imagery implies an offensive posture. As the Church moves out to defend truth, the lie will not be able to prevail, or stand, against it.

But the Church must move out. The Church should be neither silent nor stagnant.

We must not be silent, and we must not be obnoxious. The Church must proclaim, defend, and live out truth in the context of love or it is not Biblical truth—it is just another distortion.

How does the Church's mission to defend truth relate to woman's Divine design? We will consider two issues that are germane to this question.

The first issue is the responsibility of women to place ourselves under the authority and protection of the Church.

The second issue is the responsibility of the Church to women.

This chapter will deal with women's responsibility and the next chapter will deal with the Church's responsibility to women.

OUR RESPONSIBILITY

When we join a church, we place ourselves under the authority and protection of the elders (or governing body) of that church in matters relating to church-life, realizing that the Holy Spirit has guided in their selection (Acts 20:28). We enter into a covenant relationship that involves accountability.

God instructs us to: "Submit to one another out of reverence for Christ . . . Christ is the head of the church, his body, of which he is the Savior . . . (Ephesians 5:21, 23). We are also commanded to: "Submit yourselves for the Lord's sake to every authority . . ." (I Peter 2:13).

It is through submission to the ordained leadership of His Church that I place myself under the authority and protection of the Head of the Church. And we cannot have the protection without accepting the accountability and authority.

I am quite aware that to suggest to women that we should place ourselves under the authority and protection of anyone, or that we should be accountable to anyone, especially males, runs counter to everything the world is telling us. But that is just the point. The decision to join a church is not a social decision; it is a spiritual decision with spiritual ramifications.

The concept of a covenant community with God-ordained leaders flows throughout Scripture. Whereas the decision to trust in Christ alone for salvation is personal and individual, the new life in Christ is to be nurtured and spiritual gifts are to be utilized in the context of the covenant community (the Church). Scripture does not teach rugged individualism or solo Christianity. A high view of Scripture necessitates a high view of the Church.

Charles Colson and Ellen Santilli Vaughn have boldly set forth this concept in their must-read book *The Body*.[4] They state:

> Serious Christians know they need discipleship; they want to be faithful and to make a difference. But the fact is, even Christians who understand their personal identity as followers of Christ will not make a widespread difference in the decline and decay around us—unless we have a high view of our corporate identity as the body of Christ . . . Christianity is not a solitary belief system. Any genuine resurgence of Christianity, as history demonstrates, depends on a reawakening and renewal of that which is the essence of the faith—that is, the people of God, the new society, the body of

> Christ, which is made manifest in the world—the Church . . . there is no such thing as Christianity apart from the Church.[5]

Personally, I do not find this restrictive. I find it liberating. Of course the Church is not perfect (it is made up of sinners like me), but it is the impregnable institution that Jesus established to advance His Kingdom on earth.

As I *consider* the astounding truth that the risen Christ is seated at the right hand of God "in the heavenly realms, far above all rule and authority, power and dominion, and every title that can be given, not only in the present age but also in the one to come" (Ephesians 1:20-21);

And as I *contemplate* the absoluteness of His dominion: "And God placed all things under his feet and appointed him to be head over everything for the Church, which is his body, the fullness of him who fills everything in every way" (Ephesians 1:22-23);

And as I *calculate* the significance of participating in his eternal plan: "His intent was that now, through the church, the manifold wisdom of God should be made known to the rulers and authorities in the heavenly realms, according to his eternal purpose which he accomplished in Christ Jesus our Lord" (Ephesians 3:10);

And as I *celebrate* the consequences of His love: "Christ loved the church and gave himself up for her to make her holy, cleansing her by the washing with water through the word, and to present her to himself as a radiant church, without stain or wrinkle or any other blemish, but holy and blameless" (Ephesians 5:25-27);

The offers of the world pale in comparison, and the condition of submission becomes logical and pleasurable.

Again I find this liberating, for I must admit that I would be terrified to enter the spiritual battle for truth apart from the authority and protection of the Church. Jesus said that the forces of hell would not overpower His Church. To my knowledge, He has not given that kind of authority and power to any other institution on earth.

As we seek to establish ministries to reach women, and as we challenge women to fulfill our helper design by being involved in ministries of mercy, we must realize that we are moving into enemy territory. The enemy of the Church has enticed women with the fruit of self-fulfillment, and any attempt to present truth to women will be met with malicious and merciless attacks from the enemy. It simply does not make sense to do it apart from the protection of the Church. But neither does it make sense to move into enemy territory apart from the authority of the Church. Our sinfulness makes us prone to distortions. One responsibility of the leadership of a church is to guard against false teaching. I find this very comforting.

Resistance to submit to the authority and protection of Church leadership must be recognized for what it is: sin. It seems to me that this sin takes at least three forms for women today. Exploring these three forms is risky. It is particularly risky to set forth these ideas on paper. When we talk face to face I can at least answer your questions, and you can perhaps see that my honest concern is what is right before God and what is good for women (which are one and the same). I can only ask that you hear me out and that you believe that what I say is said in love.

I want to insert a qualifier before addressing these forms of resistance. I am not talking about submitting to an authority structure that is tainted with sin. If a woman finds herself in such a situation, she should seek guidance outside of that structure.

PRIDEFUL RESISTANCE

For some, resistance takes the form of pride. I can almost hear some of the voices of protest: "But Susan, you don't know the leaders in my church!"

No, I don't, but God does. And if they need to change, He is the only one who can change them. Our responsibility is not to be their conscience. Our responsibility is to pray and to participate. When there is a dearth of spiritual leadership, I always wonder if there is a shortage of praying women. By faithfully participating in Church life, we are equipped for ministry, and we have the high privilege of using the gifts God has given us for ministry.

Frankly, I grow weary of hearing people complain because their church is not alive and exciting. I have to ask the questions: Who is dead and dull? You are the church, so could you be the problem? What are you doing to encourage, equip, and enliven your church?

Again please remember that if a church is not faithful to God's Word, then it is not a true church of Jesus Christ. There are legitimate reasons for leaving a church. But fun and games are not marks of the Church. We are pathetically short on commitment today, and church hopping is a strong indicator that this is even true among Christians. The lack of loyalty is seen in the trend to attend different functions of several churches rather than attaching to one church. The self-centered attitudes of wanting my needs met and of not feeling that the church is doing what it should for me are prideful approachs to church life.

Another pride problem arises when women are unwilling to bring their Bible studies under the authority of the Church. In my work as a consultant for women's ministries in my denomination, I have many opportunities to talk with pastors. Quite often the calls come from pastors who are facing an all too common predicament. It goes something like this: "Some of the women in our church are involved in an independent community Bible study, and they want it to begin meeting in our church. Do you have any thoughts about this?"

My response to these pastors is generally something like this: Women should be willing to bring Bible study materials to the church officers so that they can determine whether or not there is theological consistency. The study materials and ministry opportunities should fit in with the overall purpose of the church and should be under the oversight of the church leadership. This does not just apply to women's studies. This is a principle that should govern all educational/ministry programs in the church, and women should not expect to be exempt.

Then I point out to the pastors some possible consequences when male officers do not give this kind of oversight. When women are involved in a Bible study that is not accountable to Church leadership, three things sometimes happen. First, if some of the doctrines of the materials being used are not in agreement with the doctrines of the Church, women may bring those teachings into the Church and create confusion. Second, women sometimes become suspicious of the spirituality of the male leadership of the Church. Perhaps this stems from being outside the authority structure of the Church, and from not understanding that men often express their spirituality differently than women. Whatever the reason, the result may be an undermining of the authority of the men. And third, these women may become isolated from other women in the Church and from involvement in the Church's ministry. If their energies are drained away from the Church's ministries, this can create tension.

I do not think that the leadership of these women's Bible studies, or the women themselves, intend for this to happen, but for some reason it sometimes does. Confusion, undermining authority, and division do not promote healthy church-life. Being aware of the possibility of these consequences in advance can alert male and female leadership to take proper precautions.

I realize that many women have sought out these Bible studies because of their deep desire to grow spiritually. But the solution is a strong and relevant women's ministry within the scope of the ministry of the Church. The Titus 2 mandate for older women to teach younger women to live godly lives was not given to women apart from the Church. In fact, it was given to the pastor of the church. It is the responsibility of Church leadership to see that there is a substantive women's ministry under the authority and protection of the Church.[6]

If you find yourself recoiling at any of this, I humbly ask you to examine your heart before the Lord and see if there is any spiritual pride, and I plead with you to consider making an investment of your spiritual gifts and knowledge in building up a women's ministry in your own church. (At least stay with me through the next chapter and consider the Church's responsibility and opportunity to reach women.)

FEARFUL RESISTANCE

A second form of resistance is fear. For some women, the very thought of submitting to the authority and protection of male leadership is absolutely terrifying. Everywhere that I speak about this topic, women come and share their stories with me. Many women have shared many stories, but often there is a similarity that is overwhelming. Women who have been abused by men, whether it was incest, rape, physical abuse, emotional abuse, or unfaithfulness, often say the same thing: "I have been attending this church for a long time, but I cannot bring myself to join. Going before the elders would paralyze me with fear, and placing myself under the authority of males is just too scary."

There are also women who have been mistreated by male leadership in a church. I am confident that in most cases it was unintentional. The men made bad judgments, and even worse, they never knew they made bad judgments. So they not only inflicted pain, but, since they were unaware of what they had done, they compounded the pain because they never apologized. The woman in this situation asks, "Would it be irresponsible for me to submit myself to the same possibility?"

The personal experiences of these women are corroborated by the dominant voices of culture (the feminists) who tell women that men are the enemies. Seeing the male-female relationship as adversarial increases the fear. And of course the sin nature kicks in and reinforces a woman's fear and resistance.

My heart breaks for these dear sisters, but their real hope is not in my sympathizing with them. Their real hope is in obedience to God's Word. It is in the church that they should find that loving authority and compassionate protection that they need. I emphasize "should" because I am aware that the church is not always a safe place for wounded people. That is the subject of the next chapter. It is a sad fact that the people in the church may not always do what is right, but that does not excuse disobedience. We as women must assume responsibility for our obedience to God. And one aspect of obedience is to become a vital part of a local church.

INDIVIDUALISM

Rugged individualism may be the American way, but in the Church, it is a third form of resistance. Self-sufficiency and self-expression are applauded in our culture. For some women, this takes on a strident insistence to "do it my way." But for many Christian women, it manifests itself quite gently. "I'm just not comfortable with form and structure. I have a passion for the poor, but it hinders me to have to work through the committees and boundaries of the church. My creativity is smothered by organization." This attitude stems from a resistance to account-ability, and it corrodes the covenant relationship that is to exist between believers in the Church. Jane Ferguson knows this, and she determined to invest her gifts and energies in serving the Lord Christ through her church in Manhattan.

A HELPER MODEL

Jane became a Christian in high school in Wichita, Kansas, and was taught by her youth pastor about the cost and value of her new life in Christ. After graduating from college with a master's degree in music, she moved to New York to pursue a career as a professional singer. She has performed throughout the country in opera, musical theater, and sacred concerts.

Spiritual dilemmas abound in a profession which breeds self-absorption and insecurity, but another dilemma called AIDS con-fronted Jane. Being a part of the performing community, she began to hear of more and more friends and colleagues, who had been active in the gay lifestyle, becoming ill. Soon the horrible disease was spreading in the IV drug users' population, into the heterosexual population, and finally to babies and unborn children. Jane was convicted by the example of Jesus' actions in Scripture that as a Christian she could not turn her back on this suffering. As she shared the love of Christ with gay friends who were ill, she began to learn the complexity of the issues surrounding AIDS and how open many of these men were to the Gospel.

Jane had a vehicle to activate her compassion. She was a charter member of Redeemer Presbyterian Church (PCA) in Manhattan. With the support of her pastor, she organized volunteers in her church and launched FRIENDS ministry to help people with AIDS. In addition to providing training for the volunteers, numerous options for ministry are offered as they network with other ministries. For example, the group cooks and serves meals at a hospice in the city for people who are homeless or are recovering from the many illnesses that affect AIDS victims. There is also a hospital visitation program, and they work with ministries to prisoners and to street people in the Bronx.

Rather than going solo to an existing ministry outside her church, Jane took her concern to her church. By investing some of her energies to equip and mobilize others in her church, she multiplied her efforts and enriched the ministry of her church.[7] This approach is more than energy efficient. The King of the Church is glorified when we "try to excel in gifts that build up the church" (I Corinthians 14:12).

DAUGHTER OF ZION . . . COME

If you are struggling with any form of resistance to placing yourself under the authority and protection of a church, the solution is simple but not easy. Recognize your resistance as sin and repent before God. Repentance will free us for the liberating experience of serving our Savior through the ministry of His Church. Dear daughter of Zion, please do not deprive yourself of the glorious joy of being a part of the Body of Christ. Whatever is holding you back from full participation in your local church, lay it aside and come . . .

. . . come to Mount Zion, the heavenly Jerusalem, the city of the living God . . . come to thousands upon thousands of angels in joyful assembly, to the church of the firstborn, whose names are written in heaven." (Hebrews 12:22-23)

The great nineteenth century theologian Lewis Berkhof stated:

In the Old Testament Jerusalem is represented as the place where God dwelt between the cherubim and where He symbolically established contact with His people. The New Testament evidently regards the Church as the spiritual counterpart of the Old Testament Jerusalem, and therefore applies to it the same name. According to this representation the Church is the dwelling place of God, in which the people of God are brought into communion with Him; and this dwelling place, while still in part on earth, belongs to the heavenly sphere.[8]

When we join a church, we become a part of the visible Church, but we also participate with that invisible host of believers of all ages in advancing the Kingdom of Christ on earth.

Now to him who is able to do immeasurably more than all we ask or imagine, according to his power that is at work within us, to him be glory in the church and in Christ Jesus throughout all generations; for ever and ever. Amen. (Ephesians 3: 20-21)

To be a defender of the Biblical truth about womanhood, the Church must be a safe place for wounded women to hear truth. How we make church safe for women is the next issue we will explore.

WOMEN
OF THE COVENANT

 Another favorite story about
brave women of the Covenant concerns John Welsh and his parish in Irongray, Scotland, during the Great Ejection period:

> On the Sunday when the non-conformists preached and bade fare-
> well to their flocks, he finished his sermon, greeted his parishioners
> one last time, and then mounted his horse. Going over to a near
> stream, he began riding up it amidst the screams and cries of his
> flock and accompanied by a bodyguard of twelve gentlemen dressed
> in scarlet. These Covenanter men, loyally bound to him by their
> saving faith in Christ Jesus, and utterly devoted to the cause, were
> seen riding off upstream with him until the entire party disappeared
> through the woods.

A new curate was assigned to the parish, but the women of the
Covenant refused to capitulate to injustice. With tears they
begged the new curate to leave and allow Mr. Welsh to return,
but to no avail. So they persisted:

> Each Sunday the women would stand behind the kirk dyke (church
> gate) and refuse to receive the new curate. One Sunday morning
> they threw stones at him. . . . In retaliation, the female ringleader
> was sentenced to banishment and the others were publicly whipped.

> Another Sunday they removed the clapper from the bell so that there
> was no means of summoning worshippers.

> They barricaded all the church doors.

> After all of this, no one came to be preached to. Those not present
> were fined one-fourth of their annual salary and one-fourth of all
> their possessions.

> Still the women fought bravely. The following Sunday they did
> attend, but each matron had a child with her. The infants began to

whimper, cry, and join each other in a chorus until the preacher was drowned out. He raved and scolded the women, but they sweetly replied that they could not leave the children untended at home!

Any women Covenanters who helped the ejected ministers and their families knew that if they were caught they would be harassed and persecuted. Nevertheless these women knew great joy in the Lord and found blessing in walking the moors traveling from one hidden Covenantal family to another delivering food, news, and comfort. They observed fasts, pleading with God for mercy for believers, and organized a conventicle (a large gathering of spiritually-minded Scottish women) in Edinburgh in 1678. These women bound themselves to this conventicle because, by it and through it, they wanted to protect the persecuted and to influence the Lords in Parliament.

These dear women not only protested the coming of so many liberal curates but refused to attend the state church services. They frequented conventicles, prayer gatherings, and fellowship times, summer and winter, day and night, no matter what the danger. Many were fined and harassed for their loyalty to the covenants. Others sheltered faithful wanderers and for doing so lost property. These godly women had to flee for their lives to the moors and the caves, often being tortured to reveal the hiding places of kith and kin. They never gave in. These ousted ministers had no more loyal friends than the women of their flocks. They were indeed a noble, devoted, and courageous group of believers.[1]

Eighteen thousand men and women died during the Killing Times. The slogan on their banners, "For Christ's Crown and Covenant," was emblematic of their supreme loyalty to the Heavenly King, Jesus Christ. The covenant these courageous heroes and heroines of the faith entered into was, for them, a binding obligation to preserve for posterity the truth of the Lordship of Jesus Christ.

ðà.   ðà.   ðà.

Chapter 4

DEFENDERS OF WOMEN

*"Keep watch over yourselves and all the flock
of which the Holy Spirit has made you overseers.
Be shepherds of the church of God, which he bought
with his own blood. I know that after I leave,
savage wolves will come in among you and
will not spare the flock. Even from your own number
men will arise and distort the truth in order
to draw away disciples after them. So be on your guard!"
(Acts 20:28-31)*

Women are responsible before God to use their spiritual gifts within the ministry of the Church, thus placing themselves under the authority and protection of the Church.

But the Church has a responsibility to shepherd women well. What does this mean?

First, because God has given men the position of authority in the home and church, male leadership in a church has the power to open ministry doors for women. Men can appreciate and affirm women. Men can make room for the gifts of women to flourish. Men are responsible for being good stewards of the resources God gives to the church, including the resource of the gifts of women. Church leadership must recognize the distinctiveness and the value of the female population of the congregation. When the nursery and kitchen are the only ministry opportunities open to women, as important as those ministries are, the Church suffers. The resulting deficiency is not because women are better, but because women are different. It takes men and women to bring completeness to the ministry of the church. The full range of the gifts and experiences of women can be utilized in the local church without violating male headship.[2]

Second, Biblical headship includes protection. One responsibility of a shepherd is to provide green pastures and quiet waters for the sheep. Today, many female sheep are bruised and battered and in desperate need of a safe pasture. They need to be protected spiritually, emotionally, and sometimes physically.

A SAFE PLACE

The primary issue of this chapter is the urgency for the local church to become a safe place for wounded women. In order for this to happen, male leadership must partner with women to care for the female sheep. The authority-protection loop can be closed when male leadership utilizes the gifts *of* women to minister *to* women.

The shepherds of the flock are entrusted with the care of the flock, and they have a responsibility to involve women in helping them understand the unique needs and vulnerabilities of a woman in distress. They have a responsibility to partner with women in caring for wounded women.

Women cannot expect men to automatically understand the plight or the passions of wounded women, but men can listen to and accept the reality of these women's situations. Often men seem to be able to "hear" better if other women bridge the gap. Spiritually mature women may be better equipped to articulate a hurting woman's pain to men, so these women can be helpers to the male leadership in a church by being the advocates for hurting women. So the reality is, the responsibility of the Church *to* women is the shared responsibility of men *and* women. And women are designed for the task. There are two compelling helper verses that accentuate this:

> The victim commits himself to you; you are the helper of the fatherless. (Psalm 10:14)

> For he will deliver the needy who cry out, the afflicted who have no one to help. (Psalm 72:12)

These verses are electrifying! Of course they do not mean that men are not to help the hurting. All disciples of Jesus are to reflect His compassion. But our female design draws us to the victims, fatherless, needy, and afflicted. God designed and equipped us with relational strengths that energize us to help others. Our femininity is fulfilled when we are involved in ministries of mercy to those who need help. And the victims, the fatherless, the needy and the afflicted are crying out for help.

There is much fallout when male-female distinctions are obliterated. First, there is incompleteness in our relationships. And second, the victims, the fatherless, the needy and the afflicted are left without the tender help that women have been created to give. There is a big hole in society because women have abandoned their calling. But far more frightening is the hollow space in our churches because women are not helping fractured women.

Today's victims, fatherless, needy and afflicted are inside and outside of our churches. It is easy to identify those outside the Church: AIDS babies, the legitimate poor and homeless, battered women, the abused, the unborn and so forth. Women who have developed a Biblical approach to these social concerns are giving wonderful leadership in their churches and communities. The nurturing instincts of women come alive when they have opportunities to minister, and it is wise leaders who tap the feminine resource in the church to touch the needs of the community.

But in this chapter I want to talk about the least recognizable of the wounded—those sitting in the pews next to us. Women who have been raped, battered, abandoned, or abused, or who have caused their own pain by having an abortion, an affair, a struggle with lesbianism, or involvement in a cult, usually think that church is the most unsafe place for them to share their hurt because they think their scars are unacceptable among such "respectable" people.

Women whose sons have AIDS, or whose daughters are anorexic, or whose husbands are alcoholics, suffer in silence because they think the women in the pew with them would consider them failures if they knew about their agony.

For many women, the pain is not in the past but is agonizingly current. They have open wounds they are trying to hide because they mistakenly think bleeding wounds are unspiritual. Some isolate themselves because they think they are the only ones having an ongoing struggle with sin.

If the Church is going to act redemptively, we must be honest about who we are—not respectable people but redeemed people, not flawless people but forgiven people.

After I spoke in a women's retreat about the need for women to make our churches safe for hurting women, a young woman lingered until others had left. She shared with me her fall into sin and the marvelous reality of God's merciful forgiveness. Her joy in her restored relationship with her Heavenly Father was obvious, but her face saddened as she told me that she still did not feel safe in church. Over and over in that brief conversation I said to her, "I am confident that God will use your experience to glorify Himself by using you to minister to others." A few weeks later, I received this letter from her:

> Last night after church I invited a single mother to go out for dessert. As we sat and talked, she told me that she has an adult child "out there somewhere," and that she has had two abortions since then. And all this happened since she has been a Christian. Her tears were dripping on the table, and I know she carries around incredible guilt. I told her what you said about church being a safe place to come and share our struggles. She admitted that she doesn't feel safe at church. She thinks people would reject her if they really knew her. How do we get past that? What can I do to help us move in that direction? By the way, being able to sit down and talk to someone about abortion and illegitimate children, and feel compassion rather than shock and condemnation, is another way the Lord has used my sin to His ultimate glory. I could not have done that until He allowed me to see the extreme corruptness of my own heart. God is so good!

We move in that direction when we recognize our corruption and rejoice in God's grace, when we refuse to be spiritual couch potatoes, when we refrain from getting caught up in the "meet my needs" syndrome, and when we resolve to share the heartbeat of Jesus: "The Son of Man came not to be ministered unto, but to minister" (Matthew 20:28).

A woman in crisis who is a member of a church should never have to wonder what she needs to do. When a Christian woman cannot trust the authority and protection of her husband, the right place for her to go is to the elders of her church. A woman whose husband has walked out on her should know that she can go to her elders for leadership. A battered woman should know that her elders will give her protection and counsel.

But that is risky. Do elders know how to handle these situations with love and compassion? And if they do handle it with love and compassion, is that putting an emotionally vulnerable woman in a dangerous situation, to say nothing of the elder?

It is a frightful experience for a woman who has been violated by a male—whether physically or emotionally abused, or raped, or if her husband has been unfaithful—to go to her elders. For her to sit in a room of men is terrifying. And often with good reason.

Glenda was kicked in the stomach and hit in the face. When she went to her pastor for counsel, she was told she must forgive her husband, go back home, and be sure he got enough sex.

Lisa's husband left her. When she went to her elders for help, they expressed their sympathy, prayed with her, and sent her home to deal with the realities of supporting her children.

When Martha told her pastor that her husband repeatedly beat her during his drunken rages, she was told that she must appear before all fifteen elders before the church could offer help. She got as far as the door but collapsed into uncontrollable sobbing at the thought of being alone in a room of men. The elders decided that her emotional instability was the real problem in the marriage.

It is also difficult for many women who have been widowed to approach church leadership for help. When Betsy's husband died, she went through tremendous turmoil dealing with the pain, the fear of parenting two teenagers alone, the realities of assuming sole responsibility for all decisions, the loneliness, and numerous other adjustments. "The cards and prayers were wonderful," said Betsy, "but I needed to know how to change a tire, and there were times when I needed money to buy the tires. There were times when I was so afraid, and I struggled with bitterness that the church was not there in tangible ways for my children and me. Perhaps I should have gone to them, but I felt so insecure and unprotected that I could not be the initiator."

You can almost hear these women echo the words of Isaiah:

> We look for justice, but find none; for deliverance, but it is far away. . . . The Lord looked and was displeased that there was no justice. He saw that there was no one, he was appalled that there was no one to intervene. (Isaiah 59:11, 15–16)

THE NEED FOR DEFENDERS

Is God appalled because there is no one in your church to intervene?

As I was becoming aware of these issues, I was appalled! I experienced a range of emotions such as denial, compassion, grief, and anger. The anger went in all directions, but much of it was towards the male leadership in churches. I would tell my husband about these women and about my frustration and anger. Over and over he said to me, "Susan, I hear what you are saying, but I must admit that I would never have imagined that a woman would be feeling that pain or having those emotions. I'm glad I have you to tell me." Finally I got the message! My husband is the kindest, most compassionate man I know. If he does not connect with female emotions without me telling him, how could I think that other men would make the connection?

Men do not intend to inflict more damage on women. Many just do not know how to deal with women in crisis appropriately and compassionately. It is difficult for men to understand the emotions of these women; but other women can be the interpreters of those feelings. When I admitted this, my emotions became productive. I realized that women, including myself, must be the advocates *to* church leaders *for* emotionally and physically bruised women. I realized that I could speak for them, and that I could encourage other women to speak for them. And I came to realize that the smallest attempt to champion their cause gives them enormous hope. Now when I have opportunities to speak to groups of men and women, I urge them to reach out to women in crisis. I receive numerous letters from women who attend my seminars. They tell me that simply acknowledging their plight gives them hope. These real letters from real women speak far more passionately than anything I could write:

> Thank you for the encouragement and validation you gave me. There are times, even now, when I respond to people's looks and their cavalier attitude toward my experiences by wondering if I really am crazy. I wonder whether other women have endured spousal battering and childhood molesting without sustaining the scars that I carry within my mind and body. I wonder if I'm making a mountain out of a molehill. Then God sends someone like you to say, "No, this really is a problem and you're not alone." It's such a relief to hear those words. Please keep saying them to women and for women.

> Thank you for what you said to our adult Sunday School class last Sunday. Your statements about abused women gave me more credibility with our church officers than I ever dreamed possible. Immediately after the class, one of the elders talked to me about forming a task force composed of women and elders to look into ministering in the area of women's issues. I could have talked until I was blue in the face and I never would have gotten through to the men in our church the way you did. Somehow hearing out of your mouth the very same things I had been telling them caused them to move me from the mental category marked "hysterical crackpot" to a category marked, "may have extraordinary insight into women's issues." I believe your willingness to give us a week-end of your life has changed the course of mine. I now have a realistic hope that I may be able to minister to other hurting women within my own church. Thank you!

Acknowledging the fact that wounded women are in our churches is the first step to freeing them from their isolation. And yet all too often the church either denies their existence or casts a shadow of doubt on their pain. I weep every time I read the following excerpts of letters I have received:

> After several years of being battered, I was finally divorced from my husband. I began attending a church and became a Christian. When I talked to the pastor about church membership, his major concern seemed to be whether I had obtained a "scriptural" divorce. He did not tell me how glad he was that I had managed to stay alive; or how brave I had been to protect my children all those years by deliberately bringing my husband's wrath down on my head whenever I saw him heading for one of my children. He didn't tell me how great it was that I had finally found the courage to leave. What he wanted to know was whether or not my former husband had actually hit me and who it was that began divorce proceedings. As soon as I assured him that my former husband had discarded me like an old shoe just as soon as it was clear to him that I was no longer willing to be a puppet suspended upon strings of fear, my pastor's face cleared and he told me that, since my unbelieving husband was the one who instigated the divorce, I was free to serve God even in my divorced state. My stomach twisted into a knot. I realized that if I had been a member of my church at the time I actually left my husband, I might not have been given the kind of advice I most needed . . . namely, get out of there and don't look back! I wanted to weep. My pastor is a wonderful, compassionate man. He cares deeply for his people . . . even the women. I have to assume that his response was born of ignorance.

> A prevalent attitude in the church is that a Christian woman will save her unbelieving husband if she just acts appropriately. A lot of people, both men and women, seem to believe it's my fault that my former husband never became a believer. Many of them want me to tell them the fatal mistake I made that ruined my witness and prevented my husband from being saved. And I have to admit that I was not particularly respectful of my husband. Respect falls way down on one's list of priorities when the list begins and ends with terror. There were many times when I lied to my husband; many times when I kept secrets from him. It was the only way I knew to survive. It was the only way I knew to keep my children safe. No one wants to hear that, and doubtless there were better ways I should have handled things if I had only known what they were.

Unfortunately, most people regard my statements about my children's safety as lame excuses for not being the kind of wife I should have been.

So many people, both in and outside the church, feel that a battered woman must really deserve it. They want to know what I did to provoke my husband's rages. I can only tell them, "Believe me, if I had been able to figure that out, I would still be married." I tried. You can't imagine how hard I tried. I've come to the conclusion that it is possible for a Christian woman not to make any mistakes and still be a battered wife. I would be so grateful to you if you would tell people that, and keep telling them until they believe it.

Women are walking in darkness. They are groping along the wall, and many are finding their way into shelters for battered women, or abortion clinics, where the arms of the feminists and the lie of the enemy are waiting for them. A woman from New Life Presbyterian Church in Escondido, California, shares with us the powerful and poignant story about her journey from being an abused wife, to the feminist movement, through several churches, and finally to new life at New Life.

SAFETY!

When I finally left my violent, abusive husband, I was relieved to make my escape, but I was so ashamed. My former husband had spent all of our twenty-year marriage telling me that his rages were my fault. If I was just a better wife, better lover, better you-name-it, I wouldn't *make* him act like that. And I believed him. Now I realize that it's difficult to be a good wife, and even more difficult to be a good lover, when you're terrified of the man you're supposed to be loving. But at the time I left him, I could only feel shame at having failed so miserably at the one and only job I ever wanted . . . that of wife and mother.

When a woman leaves an abusive husband there is generally no church, no Christian, willing to take her in. No one wants to get involved with a woman who may be "disobeying" her husband so there's generally only one place for her to go . . . a shelter for battered women. These shelters are almost always run by feminists.

Even when a woman does have another place to live, feminists are the only ones offering counseling specifically tailored to the needs of battered women. One way or another, almost any woman fleeing an abusive marriage eventually comes under the "covering" of feminists who are trained and willing to help her. As I look back at my own experience, I'm shocked to realize that churches have deserted the very women who most need them. When such a woman leaves her marriage she has no self-esteem, no idea who she is or what she believes. She is so accustomed to having someone else tell her what to do and what to think that she is nearly incapable of making decisions for herself. Her mind is completely open to brainwashing. Feminists take full advantage of that fact. They take her in. They give her empowering messages about herself and her capabilities. Then they tell her that empowerment includes the "right to choose," that the withholding of birth control (read: abortion) is a male plot to keep women subjugated. Men can't be trusted—not now, not ever. Men are after one thing—power. And a battered woman's fears underline and validate those messages.

Please don't misunderstand me. I'm extremely grateful that, in the absence of Christian assistance, feminists were there when I needed help. If it were not for feminists, thousands of women and their children would be living—and dying—in abusive situations at this very moment. Unfortunately, feminists have had to fill the vacuum left by the church. It's time for Christians to assume their responsibility in this area.

It has recently occurred to me that my sojourn in the feminist movement had a purpose. I am able to explain some of the thinking behind feminism to people who would otherwise find it inexplicable. I'm also able to point out strengths that feminists have that put the church to shame. For instance, I was loved and accepted by my feminist friends and colleagues despite the fact that I differed from them on one of their most basic tenets, abortion. (Mind you, I didn't hang out with militant feminists. My friends are "run of the mill" feminists. The kind who sense that something is terribly wrong with the way men and women relate to one another and the only answer anyone has given them for solving the problem is the feminist answer.) I always insisted on calling abortion "murder" when I was with my feminist friends. I did it deliberately. I didn't want to miss a single opportunity to draw their attention to the horror of what they are doing. At first, they argued with me. They tried to help me see that I was "selling out" half of the human race. When they discovered that my position was well thought out and not simply a knee jerk reaction, they gradually accepted it with only occasional friendly verbal sparring. Their attitude was, "You're our sister. You are one of us. We accept you, warts and all." I've received much less acceptance from my Christian friends with whom I have no fundamental differences.

One of the women with whom I most often "sparred" regarding the issue of abortion eventually wished aloud that she could afford the luxury of agreeing with me. She said, "If we weren't fighting for our lives, we would be able to be that mushy about babies, too." You see, to these women, having children means being dependent. And being dependent upon a man is dangerous because men use the power our dependence gives them in order to abuse us or, at best, they desert us.

My feminist friends know how hard I've worked to gain some mastery over my life since leaving my husband. Because they have watched me walk to the gates of hell and back they respect me as a counselor. They know that I am one who has been victimized and that I have turned my experiences into a driving force for healing in others' lives. My Christian friends seem uncomfortable with my willingness to admit I've had such serious problems in my life. I think they find it embarrassing. I have the impression that they don't want to acknowledge that women in the church could be in that much pain because they become especially uncomfortable when they realize that I was being battered while I was a member of a church.

Because my feminist friends respect me as a counselor, many of them have come to trust me with their innermost thoughts. Often, during casual conversation, these women have confided in me that they have a secret desire to find the one man in a million who might actually be trustworthy enough that they could let down their guard and share their burdens with him. Others have worried aloud that their secret desire for a man to protect them is really a sign that they are defective as human beings. A competent human being should be able to take care of herself, right? Only damaged, defective people have to rely on others for their protection . . . or so the theory goes.

Every single one of my feminist friends was abused by a man who was supposed to be her protector . . . a father, an uncle, a husband. I'm convinced that's true for the vast majority of feminists. Of course, when you think about it, that's not too hard to believe. The statistics on child abuse alone are staggering. Add to that the statistics on battered women, and you have a truly frightening picture of our culture. If you also add statistics on sexual harassment in the workplace, you're left with no more than a tiny percentage of women who have never been abused by a man. Is it any wonder these women don't trust men or that they equate "submission" with co-dependence, downright mindlessness, or worse, masochism?

I've been in church all my life. I've attended so many different kinds of Protestant churches that I used to call myself a one woman ecumenical movement. Yet, until I came to New Life I had never seen male-female relationships modeled after Biblical norms. Maybe I was just blind, I don't know. I do know that until I came to New Life I never heard a message preached that taught men that they had a responsibility to protect their wives. I would remember a message like that! In fact, I would have grabbed hold of it like a life preserver.

Something that occurred one day when I was leaving an elder's home after a Bible study will illustrate why a wounded woman may sometimes behave in bizarre ways and how others can be a help, rather than a hindrance, in her healing. When the study concluded, the elder brought all of the women's coats into the family room. I happened to look over to see my coat draped over his arm while he was helping another woman with her coat. The idea of a man coming up behind me with something in his hands with which he planned to make contact with my body—even if it was my own coat—absolutely terrified me. I knew this man was trustworthy. My reaction made no sense at all. I was gripped with fear all the same. I went over and lifted my coat from his arm. He protested, saying that he would help me with it. I tried to make light of it and joked about the fact that I live alone and am unaccustomed to valet service, but I could tell he felt put down. After I had thought about it for a couple of days and determined why I reacted that way, I called his wife and told her what had been going through my mind. I asked her to make sure he knew it was not a reflection on him. I explained a little bit about post-traumatic stress so that she would have some context in which to place my remarks. That elder and his wife have been some of my most loving supporters. I can take any prayer request to them, no matter how personal, and know that they will bring it before the Lord and not share it with another living soul. Church seems like a much safer place to me since I've developed a relationship with them.

I'm so grateful that our church has chosen to be a part of the solution rather than the problem. Because I have had the opportunity to know some trustworthy men within our church, I'm beginning to understand that God's plan for male headship may not be such a bad one after all. It's taken a lot of determination and a willingness to walk through my fear rather than running away, but I'm getting there.

More than anything else in the world I want to love and comfort broken, bleeding women. I want to be able to listen and pray with them and watch God do miracles in their lives the way He has in mine. I'm praying that the day will come when I will be able to do that under the covering of elders who actually believe that such a ministry is needed.

Some months ago, during an adult Sunday School class at New Life, I heard a lesson on submission. The elder teaching the class taught us that Christ is equal to the Father, just as women are equal to their husbands. But Christ voluntarily submits to the Father just as women need to voluntarily submit to their husbands. I thought to myself, *At last! An explanation of submission that doesn't leave me feeling like a doormat.* That lesson was so healing and released me from so much fear that it was possible for me to write the following poem.

WHEN CLOUDS WERE CAROUSELS

Once, when stars hung brighter in the sky
And clouds were shaped like carousels,
I was filled with wonder.
And the Creator, Himself, carried me to bed
On his shoulders.

I was innocent
    Full of hope. And expectation glistened
Casting rainbow colors on the future.

But monsters came in the night and stole
My innocence.
Their blackened hands left imprints on my soul.
Little rivulets of life trickled from the
Shallows there.
Year by year my soul, grown ashen,
    Lost hope. And the flame of expectation
Dwindled.

I know death. I know it intimately.
I've seen it in the mirror.
And it's stared back without shame
As if it was I who was the interloper.
Phantom-like I spent my days
Cashing in my currency for accounts receivable.
    Having only the motions of living
Without the life.

Then, a holy wind whipped
The clouds once more into carousels,
The Creator came again to carry me to bed.
And I was filled with wonder.
I had come to the end of
Myself.
And God moved in,
    Fanning the flame once more
To Life.[3]

SO WHAT CAN THE CHURCH DO?

It would take an entire book to answer that question, but here are
some starters.

- The church leadership, male and female, must make a deliberate
  decision about whether or not the church will be a safe place for
  women in crisis. This is a costly ministry. If we are going to call
  women to live in obedience to Biblical truth, we must be willing

to spend emotional and financial resources to help them. Please do not take the next steps until you take this one. It will only create more pain, because it will raise the hopes of women only to have those hopes dashed if practical help is not available.

- Use an anonymous survey to profile women in your church.[4]

- Use the information from that survey to alert the male leadership to the number of women in your own church who have had abortions, have suffered abuse, etc. Ask them to pray regularly for women in these specific situations. When the pastor prays from the pulpit for women who struggle with memories of an incestuous relationship, or for women who have been abandoned, etc., church becomes a safer place for them.

- Use the information to plan seminars addressing whatever issues surface. A strong women's ministry that is teaching women to think and act Biblically is an important component if a church is going to minister effectively to women.

- Encourage the male leadership to identify several spiritually mature women who will be available when needed to assist them in ministering to a woman in crisis. These women should be willing to keep confidences, to go with a woman to appear before the elders, to keep regular contact with the woman, and to report to the elders on her progress and needs. They should understand that they are not expected to serve as counselors, but as comforters and friends. These women should meet with the male leadership to map out a strategy and develop procedures so they will not be caught by surprise when a crisis happens. The primary function of these women would be to pray and to re-program. Women who have been treated in an evil way have lived in darkness. Their minds do not receive truth quickly. *Repetitive affirmation* is essential. They need to hear over and over that God loves and accepts them. Words such as, "You are special to God, and you are special to me," "God loves you, and I love you," "You are important to our fellowship and we need you," "Your past was dealt with at the cross—you are a treasure to your Heavenly Father," are soaked up like a sponge.

- Church members should be taught from the pulpit, and women should be taught in women's Bible studies, that the elders are

there to help wounded people and that they partner with godly
women to minister to women.

- Church members should be taught that injustice is sin and that
  submission does not mean that a woman must submit to the sin
  of abuse. Women should understand that it is wrong for a wife to
  enable a husband to continue sinful practices. She has a responsibility to him to take this to her pastor and to the elders of her
  church.

Making church a safe place is not a safe thing to do, but it is
the right thing to do. It takes courage, and I am not courageous.
The only reason I have been able to speak and write about this is
because God has called me to do it and because some of His
daughters surround me with prayer. When I think of those brave
women whose letters I have shared with you, Isaiah 62:1 burns
on my heart:

> For Zion's sake I will not keep silent,
>   for Jerusalem's sake I will not remain quiet,
> till her righteousness shines out like the dawn,
>   her salvation like a blazing torch.

We must speak for the victims, the fatherless, the needy, the
afflicted who have no one to help. But notice, we do not do it just
for them: We do it for Zion's sake, for Jerusalem's sake. We do it
for the sake of God's Church. We do it so that the King of the
Church will not be appalled, but will be honored.

But we must do more than defend women, so come with me
to our next topic as we search out ways to help them find Biblical
deliverance.

ANNA BOWDEN

The pro-life movement is not a new thing. There have been other times in history when God's people have been called to action to defend the sanctity of life:

India in the nineteenth century was no place for a lady—or at least, it was no place for an impressionable young lady, born and bred in the comfort and ease of Victorian England. It was a rough and tumble world of stark brutality and crass occultism. It was a chaotic and untamed spiritual desert.

Anna Bowden was a consummate Victorian debutante. She was a lady. But she burst fearlessly onto that awful cultural landscape with faith, hope, and love.

With a remarkable singleness of heart and soul, Anna left her family's comfortable Notting Hill social orbit of staid and privatized Anglicanism to enroll in Henrietta Soltau's mission training school in London. Formed as an adjunct to the work of J. Hudson Taylor's China Inland Mission, the school provided candidate screening and intensive preparation for women who had yielded to the call of overseas evangelization.

It was 1891 when Robert Campbell-Green, a missionary from India, visited the school. Anna immediately answered the call and soon left for mission service in India:

Her idealistic travel journal conveys the overriding vision that she carried into the work:

I know not the challenges that face me among peoples who live but for death.

I do know, though, the grace of the Savior that has called me to die but for life.

When she arrived in Conjeeveram—a seacoast town about twenty-five miles north of Kancheepuram and about forty miles south of Madras—she discovered that the mission compound of Campbell-

Green had been abandoned. Apparently, there was nothing to indicate what had happened or where the missionaries had gone. The only other English residents in the region, a small community of fabric exporters, could only say that the mission had been vacant for quite some time and that the residents of the compound had suddenly disappeared without a trace.

Despite this staggering turn of events, Anna remained undeterred. Working with the occasional and begrudging aid of the English merchants, she refurbished the mission's decrepit facilities and re-opened this tiny clinic and school.

Although most of the local residents generally maintained a cool distance, Anna's tender and magnetic personality drew innumerable children and outcast "untouchables" into her circle. After only three months, her solitary efforts had begun to reap a bountiful harvest.

It was not long, however, before Anna's jubilant optimism ran headlong into trouble. A fairly new Hindu reform movement, the *Arya Samaj*, had begun to spread in southern India. Dedicated to the purification of Hinduism and a return to the traditional values of ancient paganism, the adherents of *Arya Samaj* were bitterly anti-Western and anti-Christian. They sought a ban on "proselytism" and re-instituted such practices as *immolation* and *sarti*—the ritual sacrifice of widows on the funeral biers of their husbands—as well as *deyana*—female infanticide—and *kananda*—cultic abortifacient procedures. Although a number of very prominent missionaries attempted to adhere to the long-standing British colonial policy of non-interference—including William Miller, the renowned principal of the nearby Christian College of Madras—Anna simply could not stand idly by while the innocents were slaughtered. She immediately set up a rescue network, providing a ready escape for damned widows. And she pulled together a cadre of pro-life believers to interfere with the practices and procedures of the abortion guilds.

Describing her motivation for such drastic and dramatic activities, she wrote:

> The mandate of Holy Writ is plain. We must clothe the naked, feed the hungry, shelter the shelterless, succor the infirmed, and rescue the perishing.

I can do no less and still be faithful to the high call of our Sovereign Lord.

Apparently, her crusade began to exact a toll on the traditionalist Hindu movement because early in 1893, Swami Dayanand Sarasvati, the leader of *Arya Samaj*, appealed to Queen Victoria's viceroy to have Anna stopped. In an attempt to keep the peace, the British administrator ordered Anna to refrain from any activities that were not "directly related to the operation of the missionary outpost." Anna replied saying that rescuing innocent human life was indeed "directly related" to her mission work and that, in fact, it was "directly related to any form of Christian endeavor, humanitarian or evangelistic."

Impatient and dissatisfied with the viceroy's meek handling of Anna, Sarasvati dispatched an angry mob of his followers to the mission compound. They burned several of the buildings to the ground, raped a number of the young girls who had come to live there, and tortured and killed Anna.

But that was not the end of Anna's impact. The "clash of absolutes" that she provoked highlighted for all the world to see the unbridgeable gulf between Christian ethics and heathen brutality. Her daring example sparked a revival within the missionary community in India and her journals, published shortly after her martyrdom, made a stunning impact throughout England. Perhaps most importantly of all, her commitment stimulated and mobilized the church to call on the government to fundamentally alter the essence of the policy of non-interference—not just in India, but wherever the gospel went out around the globe—and to enforce a universal legal code rooted in the Christian notion of the sanctity of life.[1]

One woman *can* make a difference!

       ক্ষ   ক্ষ   ক্ষ

Chapter 5

DELIVERANCE

"You are my help and my deliverer; O Lord, do not delay."
(Psalm 70:5)

"The deliverer will come from Zion . . ."
(Romans 11:26)

The previous chapter was probably difficult for you to read. It was difficult for me to write. The uncomfortable reality is that "church as usual" will not do if we are going to confront our culture by ministering to the real needs of real people. We cannot act as if the people sitting on our pews live in Disney Land. They are real-world people in bondage to real-world problems. They need to be delivered from their misery.

The Hebrew word for deliver used in Psalm 70 means escape, preserve, save, rescue. Here, as well as in other passages, it is used in connection with the Hebrew word *ezer*, which means help or assistance. It is also often used in parallel with the word redeem. Redemption emphasizes payment of a price. Deliverance emphasizes release. The Greek word for deliverer in Romans 11 means to draw to oneself, to rescue, to set free.

The deliverance-redemption theme is dominant throughout Scripture. Often the Deliverer is God Himself:

> David sang to the Lord the words of this song when the Lord delivered him from the hand of all his enemies and from the hand of Saul. He said: "The Lord is my rock, my fortress and my deliverer." (II Samuel 22:1-2)

> O Sovereign Lord, my strong deliverer, who shields my head in the day of battle. (Psalm 140:7)

There are other times when God sends a deliverer:

> But when they cried out to the Lord, he raised up for them a deliverer; Othniel son of Kenaz, Caleb's younger brother, who saved them. (Judges 3:9)

> Then Jehoahaz sought the Lord's favor, and the Lord listened to him, for he saw how severely the king of Aram was oppressing Israel. The Lord provided a deliverer for Israel, and they escaped from the power of Aram. (II Kings 13:4-5)

> He [Moses] was sent to be their ruler and deliverer by God himself. . . . He led them out of Egypt. (Acts 7:35-36)

Throughout the Old Testament God delivered His people from bondage, oppression, danger, and hostile enemies. The ultimate enemy is death, and in the New Testament we see the ultimate deliverance in the life, death, and resurrection of Jesus Christ. The Old Testament stories of redemption and deliverance give us a vivid portrayal of our deliverance out of slavery to sin into the promised land of a relationship with Jesus Christ. But this deliverance is not confined to our redemption from sin:

> Unfortunately, this emphasis has become so dominant in Christian redemptive theology, there is the tendency to overlook the fact that the NT as well as the OT sees redemption, or salvation, in terms of the total human situation. Even a cursory reading of Luke's Gospel will catch the reflection of the OT heritage in the concept of salvation.[2]

MISERY TO MINISTRY

This is certainly not to minimize our need for redemption or the redemption-price paid by the Lord Jesus. The point is that the redemptive effects of His shed blood extend beyond the point of justification. That deliverance was so complete that it covers every second and every situation in the life of the person who trusts in Jesus Christ as Redeemer and King. The "total human situation" was dealt with at the cross and the tomb.

God's grace is sufficient to empower us to move from the misery of our present or past to the ministry He has planned for us.

The fruit of justification is a life of deliverance.

To act redemptively, the Church must be concerned with more than decisions for Christ. The Church must help people move from making a decision to being a disciple. And this is not an easy task when we are dealing with the victims, the fatherless, the needy, and the afflicted.

In our culture it is becoming increasingly typical for a person to come to a saving relationship with Jesus Christ who has never been in church and has no previous knowledge of Scripture.

There are scores of couples living together when they become Christians. They had never considered there was anything wrong with the arrangement.

There are countless women who have had abortions before becoming Christians without a thought that they were doing anything wrong because they were doing something legal.

There are new Christians who before their conversions had taken great pride in their homosexual relationships because their communities endorsed their lifestyle with such things as "Gay Pride Week."

Then there are those who were abused or abandoned by others. Many carry deep scars and memories. Some carry financial burdens. Some carry the AIDS virus.

These people are saved from their sin, but they bring the baggage of their past into the Church with them. Many need help in finding deliverance from the pain of the consequences of their own sin or the sin of others. They must understand that the "total human situation" can be brought to the cross. Acting redemptively means that we help them move from misery to ministry.

The Church is sometimes guilty of creating additional baggage by taking a passive approach to sin. Nonintervention does not just condone sin, it actually has the effect of promoting sin because it dulls our spiritual senses. When sin is treated lightly, it festers and infects the soul. This is why Paul confronted the Corinthian church about their sin and could then write:

Even if I caused you sorrow by my letter, I do not regret it. Though I did regret it—I see that my letter hurt you, but only for a little while—yet now I am happy, not because you were made sorry, but because your sorrow led you to repentance. For you became sorrowful as God intended. . . . Godly sorrow brings repentance. . . . See what this godly sorrow has produced in you: what earnestness, what eagerness to clear yourselves, what indignation, what alarm, what longing, what concern, what readiness to see justice done. (II Corinthians 7:8-11)

The goal of intervention is repentance. Repentance is the only way to be delivered from sin. And the goal of repentance is restoration.

Deliverance is not a passive word, and the deliverer is not one who languishes in indifference or inactivity. Deliverance implies engaging an enemy to rescue a captive. Helping people develop an integrative approach to their Christian life will involve spiritual warfare, because Satan prefers guilty, defeated, ashamed Christians rather than whole, healed, vibrant ones.

A passive, lethargic approach to church life has never been sufficient. Deliverance means involvement. You can't deliver at a distance. Denying that problems exist, or giving a quick handout, allows us to remain comfortably idle but prevents us from being what God has commissioned His Church to be.

To act redemptively, the Church will defend truth and deliver people from the distortions of truth. This deliverance is centered on the person and work of Jesus Christ. Obviously this is not the exclusive domain of women. It is the foundation of the ministry of the whole Church. But in this chapter we will focus on a slice of the ministry of rescue that women can and should be engaged in—helping Christian women in crisis to find true deliverance.

THE RISK

Making church safe for women in distress carries the risk of giving them a place to wallow in self-pity. When church becomes safe, some women find such joy in the camaraderie with other

Christian women who have experienced similar pain that they are content to be pampered. After years of isolation, the safety of sisterhood feels wonderful. So they stagnate in their own holy huddle of woe.

There is a fine line between comforting and coddling, between helping and hampering, and it is difficult to know when we have crossed over that line. But we do not give our sisters Biblical help if we allow them to remain enslaved to their misery. Neither do we help them if we escape our responsibility by sending all of them to the nearest counselor.

I am not trifling with people's emotions. There are legitimate reasons for going to a professional counselor. There are people who have been victimized. We must be very careful that we never discourage people who need professional help from seeking it. But if the Church is acting redemptively, and, in our context, if women are helping other women to face their bondage Biblically, then I don't think we will see the droves of women flocking to counselors' offices that we see today. We can minimize the need for professional help by maximizing our potential as helpers. And when professional help is needed, it will be far more efficient and effective if it is combined with the ministry of the Church. When the person in pain is a woman, it is much safer and healthier if another woman is involved in the process. Anna did not back away from such involvement.

BIBLICAL MODEL

Anna had one passion, the redemption of Jerusalem. This 84-year-old widow's longing for the salvation of God's people kept the fire in her heart stoked for over five decades as she waited, hoped, and believed.

When Mary and Joseph took the infant Jesus to Jerusalem to present Him to the Lord, Simeon was led by the Spirit to go into the temple courts. When he saw the little family, he took Jesus in his arms and praised God, saying:

> Sovereign Lord, as you have promised,
> you now dismiss your servant in peace.
> For my eyes have seen your salvation,
> which you have prepared in the sight of all people,
> a light for revelation to the Gentiles
> and for glory to your people Israel. (Luke 2: 29–32)

> Then Simeon . . . said to Mary, his mother: "This child is destined
> to cause the falling and rising of many in Israel, and to be a sign that
> will be spoken against, so that the thoughts of many hearts will be
> revealed. And a sword will pierce your own soul too." (Luke 2:34-35)

What an astounding announcement! Imagine the thoughts and emotions ignited in young Mary's mind and heart at such exhilarating and terrifying words. And at that very moment God sent a woman:

> There was also a prophetess, Anna, the daughter of Phanuel,
> of the tribe of Asher. She was very old; she had lived with her
> husband seven years after her marriage, and then was a widow
> until she was eighty-four. She never left the temple but worshipped
> night and day, fasting and praying. Coming up to them at that
> very moment, she gave thanks to God and spoke about the child to
> all who were looking forward to the redemption of Jerusalem. (Luke
> 2:36-38)

There are two ingredients of this story that must not be missed. First, the place: This event occurred in the temple. Second, the people: Simeon and Anna partnered in this ministry.

When Simeon spoke, it is likely that Mary's mind was riveted to the part about the sword in her soul—this would be enough to send any new mother reeling. But immediately Anna was there to relate to Mary woman-to-woman. Men are generally more rational and task-oriented. Women are usually more relational. Both are needed. I think this combination is evident in the Simeon/Anna partnership. They acted strategically to confront Mary with the cost of her calling, and to help her move from the misery of the sword to obedience to her mission.

THE STRATEGY

Stratagem #1: Realistic Presentation of the Cost of Our Calling

It would have been nice to talk only about the light and the glory, but mothering the Messiah would involve deep pain. Simeon knew that Mary must understand the high cost of her calling, so he did not take the easy way out.

Sometimes men avoid confronting women with the price of discipleship. I think their protective instincts take over and they hope to shield her from reality. Terri's memories of incest were creating problems in her relationship with her husband. She went to her elders and asked for their prayers and guidance. They listened to her story, commended her for coming, prayed for her, then rejoiced that now everything would be fine. These men did not intend to hurt Terri, but such an unrealistic approach caused her great confusion. Things were not all right! Terri may always struggle with those memories. They may always be her point of vulnerability. She must remain alert. She should have a plan in place to deal with this struggle. She should have been confronted with this reality, and she should have been encouraged not to feel like a failure over occasional slips.

Stratagem #2: Availability of Spiritually Mature Women to Nurture and Support

When Simeon confronted Mary with the cost of her calling, Anna moved quickly and tenderly to Mary's side to cushion the truth of Simeon's prophecy. I am fascinated at how God had older women waiting in the wings to support young Mary in her calling. Immediately after the angel's announcement that she would be the mother of the Messiah, Mary hurried to Elizabeth (Luke 1) where she found encouragement.[3] Then, after Simeon's announcement that a sword would pierce her soul, there was Anna. The parallel between what these women did for Mary is astonishing except for the fact that the same Spirit led them both.

The elders mentioned above would have been very wise to assign an older woman to meet with Terri on a regular basis to encourage and equip her to live obediently, to pray with her, and to hold her accountable.

Three basic things that an "Anna" can do for a woman with a sword in her soul are: acknowledge the sword, pray with and for her, and verbally affirm her—not just once but over and over and over.

Stratagem #3: Point to the Purpose of the Pain

Anna did not minimize Mary's pain, but she quickly reminded Mary of the purpose of her pain: The redemption of Jerusalem. Anna did not trivialize the pain Mary would endure from the sword that would pierce her soul by using therapeutic theology such as the following:[4]

- Just use these easy steps to develop a positive self-image, then you can handle whatever happens.
- Get into a recovery group and bond with people in a similar situation.
- You must learn to love yourself and then you can love those who wound you.
- Find a good counselor so you can vent your feelings.
- Read this terrific self-help book.
- Memorize these ten verses and everything will be great!

Neither did she encourage the vindictiveness that comes from seeing oneself as a victim:

- It's not your fault that you will have to endure such pain. Our culture is hostile to women.
- The real problem is that you come from a dysfunctional family, and that has caused you to be co-dependent.
- It's not fair that you should be expected to fulfill such a difficult mission.

Anna resisted these easy answers and gave Mary Biblical help by speaking about the Child who would accomplish the redemption of His people.

There was no question in Anna's mind about the certainty of God's ability and His intention to fulfill His promise of redemption. This was a done deal! She had remained unwavering for fifty years. The bedrock of such assurance is God's sovereign love. Anna did not give Mary "permission" to dwell on the pain by emphasizing the extraneous. Without hesitation she re-focused Mary on her purpose.

Mary had embraced God's glory as her life-purpose when she responded obediently to His call by saying, "I am the Lord's servant. May it be to me as you have said" (Luke 1:38). This decision now enabled her to look beyond the immediate to the eternal.

This kind of refocusing means grabbing God's promise that "in all things God works for the good of those who love him, who have been called according to his purpose" (Romans 8:28) and steadfastly holding on regardless of how long the pain persists. It is the unshakable belief that God can and will use all things to conform us "to the likeness of His Son" (Romans 8:29). This is the kind of faith that says "Though he slay me, yet will I hope in him" (Job 13:15).

Acknowledging God's sovereign love means going deep into Biblical truth. But deliverance demands moving to this dimension of truth. God's sovereignty means that He could have prevented my pain—ouch! I don't like that! If He is good, how could He have allowed such affliction? But the answer comes back from the pages of Scripture. His goal for me is far higher than external pleasure or a life without pain. He loves me so much that He desires to shape me into the very image of Jesus, and He is powerful enough to use every relationship and situation in my life to accomplish His objective. Yielding to this glorious truth delivers me from slavery to my pain—perhaps not from the pain, but from slavery to it.

Terri could have been helped toward deliverance by seeing that her pain could become her point of strength. Paul explained it when he said, "We were under great pressure, far beyond our ability to endure. . . . Indeed, in our hearts we felt the sentence of death. But this happened that we might not rely on ourselves but on God, who raises the dead. He has delivered us from such a deadly peril, and he will deliver us. On him we have set our hope that he will continue to deliver us . . ." (II Corinthians 1:8-10).

Our tendency to independence is crushed when the pressure is beyond our ability and we cast ourselves on resurrection power. Then we depend on His power that has delivered us, does deliver us, and will continue to deliver us!

Stratagem #4: Forgiveness

In speaking about redemption, Anna confronted Mary with her responsibility to forgive those who would puncture her soul with a sword.

Redemption implies forgiveness. When Adam and Eve sinned, their relationship with God was broken. But God took the initiative, went to them, and said, "I want you back so much that I will pay the redemption price." He said this realizing that the price was the life of His Son. Re-establishing that broken relationship would cost Him the dearest He had. Every page of Scripture is filled with the story of God's forgiveness which is based on the redemption purchased by Christ. One who has experienced this forgiveness is compelled to forgive others, knowing that it will never cost us what it cost God. Failure to forgive shackles. Forgiveness frees. There is no way to avoid it. Forgiveness is an imperative for one who is intimately acquainted with the Redeemer.[5]

Terri must place every ounce of her pain, every memory, every offense, on an altar and release it all to God. This does not necessarily mean there will be reconciliation with her father. It does mean that she will move towards him in forgiveness regardless of whether he moves toward her in repentance. This movement may only be emotional. If there is no repentance on his part, physical distance may be necessary.

Sometimes the hardest person to forgive is oneself. Women who have had abortions, or children they gave up for adoption, struggle with forgiving themselves. They think they are unworthy of forgiveness, and they are right—but we are all unworthy of forgiveness. That's the beauty of it. Failure to forgive oneself denies Christ's complete payment for the sin of His people.

Stratagem #5: From Misery to Ministry

For women to move all the way through their pain to God's purpose for that pain, there is another step that must be taken. I think this component of Anna's strategy is seen in the fact that "she gave thanks to God."

A sword piercing the soul and a testimony of thanksgiving would seem to be a strange juxtaposition. But pain and praise are often lined up adjacent to one another in Scripture:

> I have suffered much;
> preserve my life, O Lord, according to your word.
> Accept, O Lord, the willing praise of my mouth.
> (Psalm 119:107-108)

> . . . weeping may remain for a night,
> but rejoicing comes in the morning. (Psalm 30:5)

> He has sent me to bind up the brokenhearted . . .
> to bestow on them a crown of beauty instead of ashes, the oil
>   of gladness instead of mourning,
> and a garment of praise instead of a spirit of despair.
> They will be called oaks of righteousness, a planting of the
>   Lord for the display of his splendor. (Isaiah 61:1-3)

Paul tells us why pain and praise work in tandem:

> Praise be to the God and Father of our Lord Jesus Christ, the Father of compassion and the God of all comfort, who comforts us in all our troubles so that we can comfort those in any trouble with the comfort we ourselves havereceived from God. (II Corinthians 1:3-4)

The God of the universe is our Father, and He is able and willing to comfort us in *all* our troubles. But He does more. He uses our troubles to equip us to join with Him in His ministry of comfort. We are not just partakers of comfort—we impart comfort to others. This lifts our pain above the common to the celestial! So our reason for praise is twofold. We are comforted and we are equipped to give comfort. This praise is not just lip service. The ministry of comfort to others actually becomes our sacrifice of praise.

Until we help women to use their pain to minister to others, we have not really helped them. For the Church to challenge women to fulfill our helper design, we must help them eventually move to ministry. We do not really help them by enabling them to back away from their opportunity. I think this was Anna's gentle challenge to Mary when "she gave thanks to God."

Stratagem #6: Timing

We cannot always move people from the pain to the purpose as quickly as Anna dealt with Mary. Usually it takes longer for them to process their feelings and to appropriate Biblical truth. Timing is critical, and a helper must be in step with the Holy Spirit to know when to make this shift. The firmness of a woman's faith in God's person and promises, and her commitment to actuate her calling to glorify God, will determine the swiftness of such a maneuver. Until about five minutes ago I was struggling with Anna's rapidity. Couldn't she have been a little more patient with Mary? Then I received a telephone call.

"Susan, this is Ellinor." I had not heard the voice in several years. Ellinor had been a teenager twenty years ago when we served the church her family attended in Greenville, Alabama. Her father died very suddenly of a heart attack a few days before her thirteenth birthday. Gene and I became very involved in Ellinor's life. Her mother asked us to help her make those daily decisions of which movies Ellinor should be allowed to see, who she could date, what the curfew would be. We were delighted when the Lord brought Paul into her life. He was four years older, which at first made us a little nervous, but his love for the Lord blessed us all. While he prepared to enter the ministry he patiently waited for Ellinor to grow up and finish college, then Gene had the joy of performing their marriage ceremony.

Now Ellinor was calling to tell us that Paul had died following heart surgery. He was thirty-nine. My immediate response was, "Oh Ellinor, God is calling you to walk the same path that your mother walked." I was weeping, but Ellinor calmly responded, "Yes, but God does not make mistakes. He has never failed me and He will not fail me now." This was my cue that this was a situation where we could quickly turn from the pain to the purpose. We could immediately talk about her testimony before her children and her church. We did not sidestep the reality of the pain that would come, but we could talk about the peace that passes all human comprehension.

I had this same experience yesterday when a friend from another state called to tell me that her husband (an active member of the church) had just announced that after twenty years of marriage he did not love her anymore and was leaving. In the midst of her pain, she claimed the promises of God.

Some women grab hold of God's promises, but, like Job, feel isolated from Him. Their hearts echo Job's words:

> His hand is heavy in spite of my groaning. If only I knew where to find him; if only I could go to his dwelling! . . . But if I go to the east, he is not there; if I go to the west, I do not find him. When he is at work in the north, I do not see him; when he turns to the south, I catch no glimpse of him. But he knows the way that I take; when he has tested me, I will come forth as gold. My feet have closely followed his steps; I have kept to his way without turning aside. I have not departed from the commands of his lips; I have treasured the words of his mouth more than my daily bread. (Job 23)

Just as our experiences are different, our journeys through pain are very personalized. We cannot put the process in a box. God seems to place some women immediately in a bubble of grace. Others, like Job, are called upon to follow closely in his steps even when He does not seem to be there. The process is not necessarily an indicator of the depth of faith. We must be very careful that we never make this judgment. We must move along with a woman at the pace God is taking her.

Where possible, we must not wait until a sword pierces a woman's soul to teach her about the sufficiency of God's redemption and about her calling to glorify Him regardless of circumstances. It is likely that one reason Mary could be moved along so rapidly was the preparation she had received from Elizabeth during their three months together. Our strategy must include sound instruction in Biblical truth that will prepare women to weather whatever storms they are called to endure in whatever way God calls them to endure it, and sound assurance that if they do not depart from His commands they will come forth as gold.

ACTING REDEMPTIVELY

Mary and Joseph went to the temple. Simeon and Anna partnered in confronting Mary regarding the cost of her calling. Mary left the temple and assumed her mission of mothering the Messiah. She remained faithful all the way to the cross. Her statement at the wedding in Cana is a summary of her life. When there was no more wine for the wedding feast, Mary told Jesus the need. Then she told the servants, "Do whatever he tells you" (John 2:5). Her life was driven by unyielding obedience to do whatever God commanded.

Again, please understand that I am not saying that professional help is not sometimes needed. I am not saying that books or supportive friends cannot provide help. I am saying that these must be seen as steps along the way and that we must not get stuck at any point in the journey. The goal is not imploding self-help groups, rather it is Biblical accountability that explodes into ministry.

When the Church uses men and women to partner in ministering to women in crisis, the rational and relational strengths can be combined to help deliver women from the misery of the sword to the ministry of their calling. In the Old Testament, when the

Israelites were oppressed and cried out to God, we read, "From heaven you heard them, and in your great compassion you gave them deliverers, who rescued them from the hand of their enemies" (Nehemiah 9:27).

Jerdone Davis, a Reformed University Ministries staff worker at Clemson University in Clemson, South Carolina, tells about partnering with her local church to minister to two college students in crisis. In God's great compassion, He sent deliverers to this young couple. Jerdone tells this story with the couple's full permission:

> I received a telephone call one night from one of my girls' moms. She informed me that "our" girl was pregnant; that because she was so far away, could I be a "proxy" for this one. How could I say no? Over the last few months, this young couple has faced almost insurmountable odds, but God has proved Himself sufficient and faithful. These two, on their own, decided that the biblical thing to do would be to confess their sin to the elders of our church and then to the congregation of our church. Needless to say, they feared the treachery of such a moment, the possible rejection of Christians. Need I go on with their fears?

> Instead, they found the sufficiency of God's love expressed through the death of His only Son, Jesus Christ and through the resurrection of His life. What does that mean to this couple? Jesus took the burden, the pain, and the guilt of their sin upon Himself. He bore it so that these two did not have to. Then God raised Him from that horrible death to joyful life of eternal fellowship with God so that these two could enjoy freedom from guilt, sorrow, and pain.

> What they found was God's faithfulness expressed through a whole congregation of people who love Him. For an hour after the worship service and after their public confession, Christians lined the aisles, waiting to express their love and understanding to these two precious ones. These two, who had nothing materially, now have a home once they are married, clothes that will grow with our new "mama," and clothes for the baby when he arrives. More importantly, they know in a tangible way the love and acceptance of God's people.

A blessing that I experienced that evening was seeing true repentance take place in the lives of others of us who call ourselves Christians. People were repenting of bad attitudes, grudges they had held toward friends, bitterness, and anger not resolved. God continues even now to make our fellowship with one another sweeter, richer, and more real as the walls we have erected continue to tumble.[6]

This is a picture of the church acting redemptively!

HEALING HELPERS

When a sword pierced Mandy's soul, she also went to the church. The names in this story have been changed, but it is a real story of a church acting redemptively. Mandy writes:

> In our church, each member is assigned to an "undershepherd group" with an elder acting as the undershepherd. When the problems between my husband Mark and me escalated, my undershepherd and his wife were there for me. There was already a friendship between us, so I could go to them. I am sure that my undershepherd's wife often sensed that things were difficult, and she alerted him to specific times when I needed a call. Her involvement made it easier for me to "feel okay" about discussing this with her husband.

> When my husband left and filed for divorce, the elders were available to give me advice. They tried to meet with Mark, but he would not respond. When they asked to meet with me, they asked if I wanted a woman to come with me. I declined, but their sensitivity was comforting. They asked probing questions, and I told them the truth. Although they were very sympathetic with me, their deep love for Mark warmed my heart. There was no judgment or condemnation. Instead, they were quick to point out that, except for God's grace, any of them could have made the same wrong choices. They prayed fervently for wisdom for themselves and repentance for Mark. They agreed that I should seek legal counsel and offered to go with me to see an attorney. Their loving concern was the spiritual sheltering that I had longed for; I felt protected and encouraged. In a very real sense, they were "standing in for God" as they showed His love and mercy for both sides of this dividing home. They seemed to understand how disgusted I was that our home was seemingly being

reduced to monetary legalities but urged that I protect myself and our son. Alimony was repulsive to me. I was not even sure it was biblical. It seemed like greed. Yet these spiritually mature men gave strong Scriptural support for Mark continuing to provide. I needed this wise advice.

Our church has always provided consequences for church members who refuse to live in obedience to God's instructions. Since all members promise to live under the authority of the church, blatant refusal to obey God's laws has been met with church discipline. I was not surprised to be told that the since Mark would not meet with the elders, discipline would be necessary. My concern was our son, Bobby. He had been raised in a loving Christian home where he expected disobedience to be dealt with, so I was sure he would understand that Mark's leaving was justifiable cause for some form of response from the church. At the same time, this was his daddy. Since he would not discuss anything concerning Mark's leaving with me, I requested that an elder talk with him. One of the elders who had a close relationship with Bobby did this. Later the elder told me that he stressed to Bobby that the church was there to help us. He even told him that if Mark ever failed to send the money he was to give us, the church would take care of us. Bobby's response was, "Oh, good! . . . you know our VCR has been broken for a long time and we haven't been able to get it fixed. . . ." This was true; a VCR was not on my list of priorities! The elder took this request seriously and offered to take the VCR to have it repaired. To someone so young in the faith, a broken VCR was very significant. But more importantly, he saw that the church would take care of us.

My divorce is now final. There are so many areas of my life that are new to me. Our elders and deacons have been so helpful as I have adjusted to single life. Recently one of the men showed me how to get into the back lights of our car so that the burned-out blinker could be changed. He and his wife reinforced his advice with the invitation to bring the car to their house if I couldn't get it to work. It is encouraging to know that the elders pray for our home. I praise God for providing this church, these men, and their wives to support my son and me through this difficult time of our lives."

A postscript to this story is that this woman makes herself available to other women walking the same path. Her church took care of her, and she is now able to help care for others. She would not call herself "healed"—she is still in the process of healing. But this "healing helper" uses her experience to help others.

Ann Llewelyn is another of my heroines because this healing helper opens her wounds and walks the same path of pain over and over. Ann's pastor-husband Thom died thirteen years ago at age forty-four. Ann now works for her denomination in a ministry to the widows of pastors. This means that she re-lives the emotions and the grief time and again, but this is the ministry God has given her and He supplies the needed grace. Because she has walked the widow's path, she is a helpful helper to other women.

Our churches are filled with a cadre of wounded women whose experiences equip them to minister to others in pain. When we act redemptively, perhaps we will see these wounded women become healed helpers who move out to capture the culture for King Jesus—one hurting woman at a time.

Part II

THE DESIGN

"The Lord God said, 'It is not good for the man to be alone. I will make a helper suitable for him'" (Genesis 2:18).

As stated earlier, the Hebrew word for helper is *ezer*. Many times when this word is used in the Old Testament, it refers to God. In the following chapters, we will look at selected verses to discover some of the ways that God is our Helper. Obviously this is not all that could be said. There are countless ways that God is our Helper and countless implications about how women can help others. But as we consider selected aspects of God's ministry as our *ezer*, perhaps it will unravel some of the mystery that seems to surround woman's helper design.

It is important to remember that we do not all express the helper design in the same way. The helper design is so comprehensive and expansive that it takes all of us to do it justice. Some of us will reflect one aspect, some another aspect. We will probably even reflect it differently in various seasons of life.

There are two things that I hope we will keep sharply in focus. First, each of us is to live out this design in the particular relationships and circumstances where our Sovereign Lord has placed us. Second, each of us should render admiration, appreciation, and affirmation to our sisters who are living out this design in their relationships and circumstances. The culture is against us. We are swimming upstream. Let's not leave one another out there with no helpers. There is too much Kingdom work to be done.

> *"Rise and thresh, O Daughter of Zion,*
> *for I will give you horns of iron;*
> *I will give you hoofs of bronze*
> *and you will break to pieces many nations.*
>
> *You will devote their ill-gotten gains to the Lord,*
> *their wealth to the Lord of all the earth."*
> *(Micah 6:13)*

MARY WEBB

The date was October 9, 1800. The place was a gathering of fourteen Baptist and Congregational women. The result was the Boston Female Society for Missionary Purposes. The organizer was a handicapped woman with an indomitable spirit:

> It is not an exaggeration to assert that the hundreds of thousands of . . . local women's missionary societies, aid societies, and guilds . . . and the national denominational and interdenominational women's societies . . . all find their origin in the heart, mind, will, prayer, and action of . . . Miss Mary Webb. . . . Every Christian women's organization now in the country owes a debt of grateful remembrance to the vision, initiative, and courage of this Baptist laywoman, Mary Webb; but Miss Webb herself has vanished into the obscurity which she probably would have desired, since she sought not her own fame but rather the glory of God.

The Protestant missionary movement was about two hundred years old, but this was an era when women were excluded from active participation in the movement:

> Women could not be content with such a limited role, even in a day when it was considered preposterous for a woman's voice to be heard in church except in the singing of psalms or hymns, when none might speak publicly on any subject in the presence of men, and when they might assemble together themselves only for a tea party and social conversation. But women had played an heroic part in the Revolution. They were interested in what was happening in the world. Their religious zeal exceeded that of men generally. Girls were beginning to be educated. Women must not be denied a part in missions and they must act on behalf of their sisters in need. Yet it took tremendous courage for Mary Webb and her companions to organize the Boston Female Society for Missionary Purposes.

It was stated by one of her contemporaries that "she conducted a thousand activities from her wheelchair." Her conviction and fortitude inspired the women who met with her to join together to champion the glorious cause of spreading the light of Divine truth to other parts of the world. They decided to gather an annual collection to support the work:

> The annual dues would be two dollars. Their prime motive was that which was then dominant in missions, the giving of glory to God; and the second was benevolence and bringing the richest blessings to fellow men. The Society would consist of females who were disposed to contribute their mite towards so noble a design as diffusion of the Gospel light among the shades of darkness and superstition.

The women were well aware that they were in a strategic place. They knew that what happened in Boston reverberated throughout the land. And they were right. Soon other women took up the challenge and The Female Society was copied throughout New England and beyond:

> The parent society in Boston endeavored to give some direction to the movement. The Female Society in 1812 published in the *Massachusetts Missionary Magazine* an "address to the female friends of Zion" requesting correspondence from the other societies to be sent to Miss Mary Webb and proposing that they all meet for concerted prayer on the first Monday of each month . . . . By 1818 the number of societies in correspondence and concert had mounted to ninety-seven. Miss Webb had adapted to the women's groups the widespread practice of the friends of missions in uniting in a Concert of Prayer for Missions on a given night in each month.

> Foreign missions was the concern which for more than a century called forth the utmost devotion and effort among American Protestant women. It was for them the grand passion "all loves excelling." Here is the font of all organized women's activities in the churches and to some extent in the community. Out of the inspiration and power generated by the overseas mission there later came separate organization for home missions . . . there was this second focus of missionary concern, and home and foreign missions constantly interacted. No other form of American intervention overseas has made

a more powerful cultural impact than this work for women and children.

The Women's Foreign Mission Movement was the great cause to which American churchwomen were devoted for a century and a half.[1]

It is impossible to overlook the timing of the current downswing in this devotion to foreign missions. Surely it is more than coincidence that this decline coincided with the rise of feminism. The challenge is clear. American churchwomen must recover the vision and the vitality of Mary Webb.

ᔧ&   ᔧ&   ᔧ&

Chapter 6

HELPER-DEFENDER

"My father's God was my helper;
He saved me from the sword of Pharaoh."
(Exodus 18:4)

The helper design is multi-dimensional. Different women will exhibit different aspects of this design in various ways. The same woman may exhibit it differently in each season of her life. In this chapter, we will consider the helper as a defender in battle.

Let's begin by discussing the context of this helper verse. When Moses fled from "the sword of Pharaoh" to Midian, he married and had two sons. The names he gave these children are a statement of his condition and his creed.

When his wife gave birth to his first son, "Moses named him Gershom, saying, 'I have become an alien in a foreign land'" (Exodus 2:22).

Moses named his second son Eliezer, "for he said, 'My father's God was my helper; he saved me from the sword of Pharaoh'" (Exodus 18:4).

Moses gives a clear statement of his condition: He was an alien in a foreign land. He also declares his doctrinal creed: The God of his father, the God of Israel, the God of covenant faithfulness, was his helper. In the words of John Calvin, "by their names he was daily reminded that God's covenant was to be preferred to all earthly advantages."[2]

This aspect of the helper design suggests a recognition that Christians are aliens and have enemies, and that they have a resoluteness to defend the people of God against the pharaohs of those enemies. So the question is, what shape and form does this put on women's ministry of help? As I thought and prayed about this, I was drawn to an account of the New Testament Church facing the sword of one of its enemies' pharaohs. And in this story it was a woman who went to battle to defend the servant of the Church against the enemy of the Church. It was a woman who confronted the hostile culture fully aware that she was also involved in a spiritual confrontation.

A BIBLICAL MODEL

In Acts 12:1–5, we read that "King Herod arrested some who belonged to the church, intending to persecute them. He had James, the brother of John, put to death with the sword. When he saw that this pleased the Jews, he proceeded to seize Peter also . . . he put him in prison. . . . Peter was kept in prison, but the church was earnestly praying to God for him."

The night before Herod was to bring Peter to trial, Peter was sleeping. Herod's track record in trying believers was not good. There is no doubt that he intended to kill Peter. Yet Peter was experiencing that "peace of God, which transcends all under-standing . . ." (Philippians 4:7).

That is amazing but not surprising, because the Church was acting like the Church. The Church was neither passive nor panic-stricken; the Church was praying and Peter was peaceful. Peter had internal deliverance even as there were external chains.

But there is more. Peter was delivered from the sword of Herod:

Peter was sleeping between two soldiers, bound with two chains, and sentries stood guard at the entrance. Suddenly an angel of the Lord appeared and a light shone in the cell. He struck Peter on the side and woke him up. "Quick, get up!" he said, and the chains fell off Peter's wrists. Then the angel said to him, "Put on your clothes and sandals. . . . Wrap your cloak around you and follow me." . . . Peter followed him out of the prison, but he had no idea that what the angel was doing was really happening; he thought he was seeing a vision. They passed the . . . guards and came to the iron gate. . . . It opened for them by itself, and they went through it. When they had walked the length of one street, suddenly the angel left him. Then Peter came to himself. (Acts 12:6–11)

What happened next is absolutely fascinating. "When this had dawned on him, he went to the house of Mary the mother of John, also called Mark, where many people had gathered and were praying" (Acts 12:12).

We are told earlier that the Church was praying. Quite likely the Church had gathered in many homes throughout the city. But it is now the middle of the night. Why did Peter go to Mary's home?

Perhaps Peter suspected that most of the prayer meetings ended at a decent hour, but he knew that Mary would have persevered. Apparently he had full confidence that she would have recognized the urgency of this crisis. She would have known they were in a spiritual battle, and she would have done what needed to be done. Mary would have gathered believers to pray, and she would have continued to defend in prayer as long as the conflict continued. Mary knew there was no time for protests or petitions. The exigency of this battle required intercessory prayer. Peter did not have to wonder where he should go. He knew Mary's reputation as a prayer warrior because this must have been her practice. What a reputation!

This amazing story of Peter's deliverance is an illustration of the same truth that Moses expressed in his statement of his condition and his creed: Believers are aliens in this world; God is our Helper. To understand the implications of this truth, we must get beneath the obvious facts of Peter's deliverance story and probe the spiritual significance of these events.

First, we must understand that Peter could not free himself. He was a helpless prisoner chained to two soldiers with other soldiers standing guard at the entrance to his cell.

Second, the order of the events is critical to understanding the significance of the events. A light shone in the cell, Peter was commanded to action, the chains fell off, and Peter followed. This is a picture of sovereign grace.

Unbelievers are in a helpless condition. They are bound with the chains of sin. They are "dead in transgressions and sins" (Ephesians 2:1). To command them to action is as ridiculous as it is to command a dead man to action. Before there can be the action of faith there must be light. The light is the regenerating power of the Holy Spirit. Regeneration is the only power that can loose the chains of unbelief. Once that light shines, the chains of unbelief fall off and the unbeliever is empowered by the Holy Spirit to repent and believe. People in prisons of unbelief need defenders who will intercede before the God of all grace on their behalf. Intercession is one expression of the helper design.

DEFENDING IN PRAYER

Anita told me that she was determined to debate her unbelieving husband into the Kingdom. She spent every day preparing her arguments and every night erecting barriers as she presented her brilliant rationale. She finally came to understand that this approach ignores the helpless condition of the sinner and relies on the power of human persuasion. The person in chains needs the light of grace. Only God can shine that light into the depths of unbelief, command the action of repentance and faith, and loose the chains so that the person is able to follow. The crisis of unbelief demands intercessory prayer. When Anita began spending her time and energy praying rather than preparing arguments, God intervened and drew her husband to Himself.

But often it is a believer who is in the chains of his or her own sin. Perhaps it is a daughter bound by a sinful relationship with a non-Christian boyfriend, or a son addicted to drugs or pornography, or a friend chained to an unforgiving spirit, or male leadership in a church tied to a complacent or a controlling spirit. Nothing less that the power of grace can work the deep repentance that is needed to unloose those chains.

Or perhaps the situation is similar to Peter's predicament. Maybe it is a husband in jail for protesting the murder of unborn children, or a mother shackled to a cancerous body, or a college student being threatened with failing her course in feminist studies because she wrote a paper on woman's helper design, or a church experiencing unexplainable problems and difficulties on all sides.

Whatever the situation, the power of God is our hope, and relentless intercessory prayer accesses us to that power.

In spiritual warfare, the weapon is prayer. A humanly impossible situation is prime time for intercessory prayer. A helper who desires to defend another against the pharaohs of this world knows that this battle is fought on two levels:

> For our struggle is not against flesh and blood, but against the rulers, against the forces of evil in the heavenly realms . . . pray in the Spirit on all occasions with all kinds of prayers and requests. With this in mind, be alert and always keep on praying for all the saints. Pray also for me, that whenever I open my mouth, words may be given me so that I will fearlessly make known the mystery of the gospel, for which I am an ambassador in chains. Pray that I may declare it fearlessly, as I should. (Ephesians 6:12, 18-20)

In this struggle against the forces of evil, intercessory prayer is essential. Prayer is the weapon that will move us above the cultural level of what is seen to the spiritual level where the real insurrection is taking place. It is through prayer that we fight those unseen forces of evil. Chuck Colson has said it well: "When the Church transcends culture, it can transform culture."[3]

We transcend culture when we confront the unseen enemy in prayer.

In her inimitable way, Edith Schaeffer says:

> The staggering reality is that each of us has an opportunity to affect the battle in the unseen world, as well as what is going on in neighborhoods, villages, portions of towns and cities, states, the nation, or other parts of the world. To shrug our shoulders and say, "I don't matter," is not to be humble, but to be unfaithful to what the Lord has for us to be doing in prayer in trusting the Lord, as well as in

being what we are meant to be as an influence. It could be any-
where—in our wheelchair, our hospital bed, our cell where our cap-
tors put us, our tank, our pilot's seat on a plane, our tractor, our
kitchen sink, our vegetable garden, our teaching place with a few
young children or Ph.D. scholars, our "march for life" as things are
being thrown at us, our adoption of a pregnant woman for a period
of time or a child for a lifetime.[4]

Help implies the initiative of a helper. This is demonstrated in
a fascinating way in the book of Hebrews:

For surely it is not angels he helps (*epilambano*), but Abraham's
descendants. For this reason he had to be made like his brothers in
every way, in order that he might become a merciful and faithful
high priest in service to God, and that he might make atonement for
the sins of the people. Because he himself suffered when he was
tempted, he is able to help *(boetheo)* those who are being tempted.
(Hebrews 2:16-18)

The first word translated help, *epilambano*, means "to lay
hold of." Our English word lacks the fullness and majesty to
convey what actually happened in the act of God becoming like
us, and not like the angels. But what is important to see here is
that the whole act of God laying hold of our flesh resulted in
eternal help to us; grandest yet prosaic, everyday help. The same
word is used when Christ reached out to Peter as he was sinking
in the waves (Matthew 14:31). Here again Jesus is taking hold of
man in a deliberate, decisive, compassionate action of help.

The second word translated help, *boetheo*, means "to come to
the aid of, to succor, to relieve." Because Jesus laid hold of our
flesh and became like us, He is able to come to our aid when we
are tempted.

The helper who is called to defend through intercessory
prayer understands that she must lay hold of the promises and
power of God in a deliberate, decisive, and compassionate action
of help in order to come to the aid of those in chains. She knows
that these battles will not be won with human persuasion or protests, but by Divine power. The helper echoes the words of the

Psalmist: "Some trust in chariots and some in horses, but we trust in the name of the Lord our God" (Psalm 20:7).

In his book *Prayer Shield,* Peter Wagner gives an interesting twist to the ministry of intercessory prayer. He explains that whereas intercession is expected of every Christian, some people do seem to have a special ministry of prayer, or gift of intercession. He goes on to say that there seems to be a higher percentage of women with this gift:

> It was interesting to discover that all of those with the gift of intercession in my class were women. This is not unusual. I have not as yet done enough research to come up with a firm figure, but my observations over the years lead me to guess that 80 percent of those with the gift of intercession are women, across theological and cultural spectrums.
>
> I have found that certain spiritual gifts seem to be biased by gender. . . . But why would more women be intercessors? Psychological profiles in general have shown women to be more intuitional and men to be more rational. Some intercessors themselves have suggested that a woman's biological function of conception, gestation and the travail of giving birth might have something to do with it. A major ministry of intercessors is to bring into being the purposes of God, and many describe some of their more intense periods of intercession as travail. Mothers know even better than could the apostle Paul the full meaning of his statement, "My little children, for whom I labor in birth again until Christ is formed in you" (Gal. 4:19).[5]

I would add one more spin to Wagner's assessment that there is a higher percentage of women with the special gift of intercession. My unscientific observation is that of the women with this gift, a high percentage are widows. It seems to me that widows have entered into a dimension of dependence on God that prepares them for the ministry of intercessory prayer. The widow's mite was recognized and commended by Jesus because "she, out of her poverty, put in everything—all she had to live on" (Mark 12:44). Perhaps the widow's "might" is most mighty when these women band together as helper-defenders in intercessory prayer. Older women who do not have the daily responsibilities of families or jobs are another power source for intercessory prayer. Since I have been speaking against the distortions of truth, I have encountered the fury of the enemy. But I am convinced that the prayers of women who have taken up this cause on their knees have built a hedge of protection around me.

The relational strength of our helper design causes women to attach fiercely to people and purposes. We don't turn loose easily. This tenacity equips women to persevere in intercessory prayer for years. Countless mothers have prayed for wayward children long after others lost hope. I have often wondered about the mother of the prodigal son. There is no mention of her in that parable, but could it be that in that spiritual altercation for his soul, it was the prayers of his mother that caused the light to shine in his heart and the chains to fall from his will even as he was up to his knees in the mud of that pig pen?

PRAYER WARRIORS

Mrs. Johnson was one of my spiritual mothers. When my husband was pastoring a small group of people trying to begin a church, Mrs. Johnson was one of our members. We met in a storefront, and it was exhilarating but exhausting work. Even before the infant church was able to purchase property and move to a permanent building, Mrs. Johnson was confined to a nursing home. From her bed she continued to be our cheerleader. At times when I did not think I had energy to continue, I would go and sit by her bed and get refueled. She taught me many lessons, and she was always full of surprises. But one day she startled me when we were talking about preachers that she enjoyed watching on television, and she said, "But I never watch any of the services on Sunday mornings." When I asked why, she simply said, "Because I am praying for my own church and my own pastor as you gather to worship our Lord." Then I understood why our little church was surviving and growing despite ferocious attacks from the enemy.

Fae Allen is an intercessor for missionaries. Now eighty-six, Fae's initial exposure to praying for missionaries happened about twenty years ago when she noticed a display of missionary prayer cards. She selected one of a single lady working in Guatemala and began a correspondence with her as well as praying for her. Fourteen years ago she was asked to be the Missions Chairman for the women's ministry in her church. Part of the job was to read, edit and print letters from missionaries supported by the church. The love affair began in earnest. "When you read those letters, you can't help but get involved. You feel for those people—you pray for them," Fae explains. Her prayer time begins early in the morning, but she finds that the Holy Spirit brings individuals and needs to mind all during the day . . . and sometimes the night. "I don't seem to have any trouble remembering their names, when often I can't recall the name of my neighbor," she said. She keeps up with more than fifty missionary families and reads every letter they write to the church, answering them as she senses a special need or just a word of encouragement. Only in eternity will Fae and those she has prayed for know the battles they fought together.

Pastor Glen Knecht tells of going to the Ukraine after the fall of communism and attending a church service. "How mistaken the Communists were when they allowed the older women to continue worshipping together! It was they who were considered no threat to the new order, but it was they whose prayers and faithfulness over all those barren years held the church together and raised up a generation of men and young people to serve the Lord. Yes, the church we attended was crowded with these older women at the very front, for they had been the stalwart defenders and maintainers of Christ's Gospel, but behind them and alongside them and in the balcony and outside the windows were the fruit of their faithfulness, men, women, young people, and children. We must never underestimate the place and power of our godly women. To them go the laurels in the Church in Ukraine!"[6]

Halfway around the world, essentially the same thing that happened in the Ukraine happened in Lookout Mountain, Tennessee. In 1973 the Holy Spirit visited the Lookout Mountain Presbyterian Church in a magnificent manner. People, including church officers, were converted; there was a renewed sense of urgency in reaching the lost at home and around the world; and people made life commitments that continue to bring glory to the Lord God twenty years later. Pastor Sanders Willson is convinced that this lasting revival occurred because of a small women's prayer band that met every week for seventy years. I am convinced that what happened in the Ukraine and on Lookout Mountain has happened around the globe throughout history. One of the thrills of heaven will be to discover how the Father blessed the prayer power of His daughters.

Consider these words, penned over a hundred years ago by our sister who wrote *The Women of Christendom:*

> The warfare of the Christian Church continues still. "Militant here on earth" is the title she bears, not in one age or in one country only, but everywhere and always. . . . If this warfare against evil, in individuals or in a body, is forgotten for a time, it will be found that it is not because the victory is complete, but because the good soldiers are slumbering: and in the slumber the foes, who never slumber, are stealthily gaining ground. . . . The real essential battle-field is, we must remember, always in the heart itself. It is the victory over ourselves, over the evil within, which enables us to gain any real victories over the evil without. . . . Every good life in this world is and must be a warfare. What makes it good is that the warfare is a conquest.[7]

The daughter of Zion who is diligent in holding off the enemy in her own heart will have a freedom to wage war on behalf of others. This woman has learned that she has an Intercessor at the very right hand of God who "intercedes for us with groans that words cannot express" (Romans 8:26). Because she is intimately acquainted with the Intercessor, she is empowered to be a helper-defender. What a glorious calling!

> You may see her in the grocery with her children
> Or in the city nine to five each working day

She's a mother or a teacher or a woman all alone
But she's something else entirely when she prays.

We don't see her lonely nights of intercession
Or the tears she sheds with every whispered prayer
We may not see the secret things hidden in her heart
But the eyes of God are watching her with care.

She's a prayer warrior down on her knees
Wrestling with powers and principalities
Standing in the gap for others
For her sisters and her brothers
Reaching heaven with her heart.[8]

CATHERINE TAIT

Even as a young girl Catherine Spooner had a deep love for Christ and a desire to serve Him. She once told a girlhood friend of hearing in her heart the message, *make for the higher.* She was still quite young when she became the wife of the headmaster of a school for boys from wealthy families:

> Seventy boys lived in her husband's house and hundreds were educated in the great school, and lived near. And, young as she was when she married, her motherly kindness was felt throughout the house and the school.

> The poor came to her house and were wisely succored. They loved and respected her much, and she established a school for their children, in which she taught every day.

> On half-holidays she was always with her husband, riding with him along the green country lanes and over the meadows.

> She was the chosen companion of her husband's thoughts, as well as the rest of his heart. They both delighted in natural beauty. Her mind was stored with the Sacred Scriptures, and with passages from our great poets, which would flow forth in their walks together among the hills.

When her husband was transferred to the Deanery of the cathedral in Carlisle, she continued her work among the poor. It was during these years that she gave birth to seven children:

> Her husband writes of her: "It was one of her chief characteristics to find enjoyment in any duty she had to perform. There was in her no trace of the fine lady who thinks her husband's common work a thing in which she need not take much interest. Her heart was in all we had to do together, and in all my separate work. While she found time for her own labors among the poor, and her own reading, her deepest interests were ever mine. . . .

God gave her wonderfully good health, and she had a natural joyousness and buoyancy of spirit, which in her girlhood often made her laugh to herself for happiness.

And yet, through this life of activity and prosperity and social intercourse, deep in her heart rose a spring of deep communion with God, fed through the public services of the Church, by private prayer, and by the living, intelligent, continual study of the Holy Scriptures.

And so, when again and again, as it happened to her in the wonderful education of God, this life of activity was suddenly overspread by the shadow of dangerous illness in those she loved, or rent asunder by a chasm of death, she was ready; and, rooted in the love of God, through all the tempest of sorrow stood as unselfish and strong to sustain others through the storm, as she was bright to gladden them in the calm.

. . . sorrow came on the full bright home at Carlisle, wave after wave, all but overwhelming and sweeping the whole beautiful, ordered, living, happy home-world away. . . . Another babe was born into that happy home, and before the little one they all welcomed as their pet and darling was a month old, one after another of that bright little band began to fail with mortal sickness. . . . Within five weeks the five lovely little sisters had all sickened of scarlet fever and died.

And to the bereaved parents none were left but the only son and the baby of a few weeks old.

Through all their anguish of sorrow, the mother and father never failed to sustain their beloved little ones with prayer and tender watching, and holy words of God, to the very last. . . . "Thus were we called to part with these five most blessed little daughters, each of whom had been received in prayer, borne in prayer, educated with prayer, and now given up, though with bitter anguish, yet with prayer and thanksgiving."

Soon after this desolation of their home, they were removed to what was the third and last stage of her earthly life, her husband being called successively to the Bishopric of London and the Archbishopric of Canterbury.

The terrible devastating storm had not made life empty to her, because she was still in one kingdom and service with her beloved; and the work she loved best was the work of serving and succoring, which is the life of heaven.

After this followed twenty years of ceaseless, fruitful labors in the bright Christian home, again filled with four children . . . that home which was a welcoming place for the whole English Church, and more, and which helped to diffuse through the charities of the largest city in the world the natural and personal kindliness of home. She never lost her personal sympathy with individual sufferers in the extent of the institutions she founded and ordered so wisely.

All her good works seem to have grown naturally out of present needs. Her Orphan Home arose from a day's visit to the east of London, where numbers of little children had been left orphans at the time by a terrible outbreak of cholera. . . . She also founded a Ladies' Diocesan Society, which gathered together the women of rank and wealth who only live in London during the session of Parliament and the Court season, to unite in giving a regular portion of their time to assist the poor of the metropolis, assigning to each lady some workhouse, or hospital, or refuge, or orphanage, or some poor families to attend to.

And yet, with all the strain of this large organization, she could always find time to enter heart and soul into the individual troubles of one and another of the ladies themselves who came to her, lifting up her heart in intercessory prayer, the fervency and fitness of which years could not efface from the memory of the one so succored.

A friend said that the most characteristic thing about her was the way she spent the Sabbath. She related that when you met her on Sunday morning, her face radiated the fact that it was her "day of days."

And an aged American bishop who visited them wrote of their every-day life: "I delight to stay with these people. From early service in the morning to the late prayers at night, life seems always in God's presence."

And so the beautiful, fervent, ordered life went on, nourished by the old familiar springs . . . by the Holy Scriptures, and by prayer.

Until at last the last sorrow came, and sent her home.

The one son . . . grew up to twenty-nine. The love between the mother and this only son was most devoted. His early, never-forgotten lessons in the Bible were mostly from her. She entered into his historical reading while at the University. He consulted her in every difficulty and trouble, and was the hope and joy of the home.

And at nine and twenty, when life was opening in widest usefulness and hope before him, after months of lingering illness, he died.

The bereaved mother stood for one moment alone at his grave, when the burial was over, and said, in a low but intensely earnest and thrilling voice, heard only, it is believed, by one young relative, "I believe in the Resurrection of the dead."

"None but my God and I know what I have suffered," she said softly to a trusted friend.

She by no means shut herself up with her grief. She went about doing her daily work as courageously as ever. But the change which sorrow wrought upon her countenance, her furrowed cheeks and rapidly whitening hair, told what had else been almost untold. . . . Six months after her son's death, the unfailing, vigorous health gave way, and she died.

She was perfectly calm and collected in her last moments. She spoke of her five and thirty years of wedded love. She said she wished to live a little while, for Christmas would be sad without the mother. Her husband administered the Holy Communion to her, to the daughters, and the physician. When his voice faltered in the hymn, "Jesus, Lover of my soul," her voice supplied the missing words.

Once more he offered beside her the beautiful Commendatory Prayer they had said together beside their five children. And soon afterward her breathing ceased, with a gentle sigh.

She had gone home to the Father's house, of which her own earthly home had been such a lovely type; the Father's house, which is the centre of love and succor to the whole world.[1]

ða   ða   ða

Chapter 7

HELPER-SUPPORTER

*"May He send you help from the sanctuary,
and grant you support from Zion!"
(Psalm 20:2)*

Psalm 20 is an intercessory prayer
on the part of the nation for King David. Some believe that it was
written during the time of his sinful encounter with Bathsheba,
which left him sick in body and soul as he himself records in
Psalm 51:

> Have mercy on me, O God . . .
> I know my transgressions, and my sin is always before me.
> Against you, you only, have I sinned and
>   done what is evil in your sight . . .
> Let me hear joy and gladness; let the bones
>   you have crushed rejoice . . .
> Restore to me the joy of your salvation and grant me a willing
> spirit, to sustain me.

It is obvious that David was in a spiritually vulnerable condition. Though he was at the peak of power, he was in the depths of
defeat. In that context the people prayed:

> May the Lord answer you when you are in distress;
> may the name of the God of Jacob protect you.
> May he send you help from the sanctuary
> and grant you support from Zion. (Psalm 20:1-2)

The plea for protection, help, and support from the sanctuary,
from Zion, indicates that David's real need was a spiritual need.
David needed protection from the evil one who is quick to take

advantage of our vulnerabilities. He needed the help of God's Spirit to be restored in his inner being to the joy of intimacy with God. He needed the help of God's Spirit to give him a willing spirit to do what was right and to sustain him as he moved in obedience.

David was in need of a Helper to protect and support him in his time of weakness.

The word protect means "to set securely on high."

The Hebrew word translated support means to sustain, to uphold, to refresh.

There is an interesting verse in Psalm 144: " . . . our daughters will be like pillars carved to adorn a palace" (Psalm 144:12).

A pillar, according to the dictionary, is "a . . . support; one who occupies a central or responsible position." Some of the meanings of the root Hebrew word that is used here are: to attend, to defend, to give stability, to join. The ideas of protection and support are clear in this imagery.

In summary, a helper supports by protecting, sustaining, upholding, refreshing, attending, defending, and stabilizing.

It seems to me that nowhere is woman to exhibit this aspect of her helper design more clearly than in the marriage relationship. Not every woman is called to marriage, but this is a primary relationship for most women and one that surely should be addressed in any attempt to understand woman's creation design. The woman who is not married should understand this concept so that she can be a helper to women who are married. And widows have a hindsight perspective of this concept that qualifies them to "train the younger women to love their husbands . . ." (Titus 2:4).

It also seems to me that there is probably no aspect of our design that is under more attack, which means that the marriage relationship gives women a supreme opportunity to make a difference in our culture.

Recently I sat on the first pew in our church and watched our youngest daughter, Laurin, become Mrs. Scott Coley. It was a joyous event. I cried when I stood and turned to watch that beautiful young woman walk down the aisle on the arm of her dad. I cried for joy that our baby had become such a godly woman; I cried in gratitude that God had answered the deep prayer of our hearts in giving her a Christian husband; and there were some tears of reality that Cinderella's coach would turn into a pumpkin! Real life is not the fantasy of a lovely church wedding. The first week after their honeymoon they both had a stomach virus— Cinderella's ball was over!

But worse than a stomach virus is the reality that I tell the young adults in my Sunday School class: When you get married, you step to the front lines of a war zone, and the enemy is not your mate. It often feels as if your mate is the enemy, but that is because the real enemy of your marriage knows the effectiveness of the "divide and conquer" strategy. The war zone is the battle between light and darkness, the enemy is Satan, and one of his prime targets is marriage. The only way you will survive this conflict is to recognize and stand together against your common enemy and to embrace the American Dream. Hold on, I am not talking about the modern version of that dream. I am talking about the *original* American Dream.

The preamble to the Mayflower Compact states:

> We, whose names are underwritten . . . having undertaken for the glory of God and advancement of the Christian faith . . . a voyage to plant the first colony in the northern parts of Virginia.

William Bradford, the first governor of this colony (Plymouth), wrote:

> Last and not least, they cherished a great hope and inward zeal of laying good foundations, or at least of making some way towards it, for the propagation and advance of the gospel of the kingdom of Christ in the remote parts of the world, even though they should be but stepping stones to others in the performance of so great a work.[2]

The original American Dream of propagating and advancing the Gospel of the Kingdom of Christ in every remote neighborhood, apartment building, suburb, mobile home park, condominium, and retirement village in our country should be the "cherished hope and inward zeal" of Christian couples.

With the wholesale dismantling of families, providing "stepping stones" for the next generation to know what a "till death do us part" marriage looks like should be the vision of Christian couples.

Michael and Brenda Anthony maintain this kind of focus and vision for their marriage by writing each other a love letter each year. In these letters they restate their hopes and dreams for their marriage. This tradition began when they had no extra money and Michael was unable to buy Brenda a birthday gift, but what a rich legacy these letters will be for their children.

The great need of the hour is women of substance who will rise above the shallowness of self-centeredness and support their husbands, women of courage who will take the risk to do the right thing even when it is the hard thing in order to protect their husbands, women of noble character who will love their husbands Biblically even when it is difficult.

A MOTHER'S ADVICE

The mother of King Lemuel knew the value of a virtuous woman, and in Proverbs 31 she exhorts her son to search for such a wife. She begins by explaining why it was so strategic for him to make a wise selection of a life partner:

> O my son, O son of my womb.
> > O son of my vows,
> do not spend your strength on women,
> > your vigor on those who ruin kings.
> It is not for kings, O Lemuel—
> > not for kings to drink wine,
> > not for rulers to crave beer,
> lest they drink and forget what the law decrees,
> > and deprive all the oppressed of their rights . . .
>
> Speak up for those who cannot speak for themselves,
> > for the rights of all who are destitute.

> Speak up and judge fairly;
>> defend the rights of the poor and needy. (Proverbs 31:2-3)

You can feel the passion in this mother's plea to her son. And I have to believe that her plea was consistent with her performance. She had lived a virtuous life before him so her exhortation was credible. It seems to me that this mother understood her son's need for a virtuous woman because she had a clearly defined perspective of woman's helper design.

Her son was not called to a life of self-indulgence. Her son was called to remember God's law, to protect the rights of the oppressed, to be an advocate for the destitute, and to defend the rights of the poor and needy. Her son was a king, and he must act kingly. And a helper-supporter was essential to help him fulfill his calling.

It is as though she is saying, "If you spend your strength on a lesser woman, she will be your ruin. But a woman of noble character will enable you to accomplish these noble goals. You need a virtuous wife to be what you have been called to be." I know this conversation well. I had it with our son Richie many times, and I was never sure he heard a word I said until he told us he was going to marry Shannon. Then I knew he had listened. She was all I had prayed for and had told him he needed! So mothers, take heart and keep having this conversation with your sons.

Lemuel's mother then described a woman of noble character and explained why she is "worth far more than rubies." (You get the feeling that she knew he would never figure this out for himself—it took a mother to spell it out!)

> A wife of noble character who can find?
>> She is worth far more than rubies.
> Her husband has full confidence in her
>> and lacks nothing of value.
> She brings him good, not harm,
>> all the days of her life.
> She selects wool and flax
>> and works with eager hands.

She is like the merchant ships,
> bringing her food from afar.

She gets up while it is still dark;
> she provides food for her family
> and portions for her servant girls.

She considers a field and buys it;
> out of her earnings she plants a vineyard.

She sets about her work vigorously;
> her arms are strong for her tasks.

She sees that her trading is profitable,
> and her lamp does not go out at night.

In her hand she holds the distaff
> and grasps the spindle with her fingers.

She opens her arms to the poor
> and extends her hands to the needy.

When it snows, she has no fear for her household;
> for all of them are clothed in scarlet.

She makes coverings for her bed;
> she is clothed in fine linen and purple.

Her husband is respected at the city gate,
> where he takes his seat among the elders of the land.

She makes linen garments and sells them,
> and supplies the merchants with sashes.

She is clothed with strength and dignity;
> she can laugh at the days to come.

She speaks with wisdom,
> and faithful instruction is on her tongue.

She watches over the affairs of her household
> and does not eat the bread of idleness.

Her children arise and call her blessed;
> her husband also, and he praises her:

"Many women do noble things,
> but you surpass them all."

Charm is deceptive, and beauty is fleeting;
> but a woman who fears the Lord is to be praised.

Give her the reward she has earned,
> and let her works bring her praise at the city gate.
> (Proverbs 31:10-31)

Let's consider some of the benefits of marrying such a woman that Lemuel's mother presented to her son.

SUPPORT BENEFITS

Benefit #1

A husband married to this kind of woman "has full confidence in her and lacks nothing of value." The Hebrew word translated confidence also carries the idea of trust, security, and safety, which lines up with the calling of a helper to support and protect. This should cause every Christian wife to ask some piercing questions. Does my husband know that I protect his reputation by never criticizing him before others? Does he know that even when he fails, I will be there to cushion his fall? Does he know that no matter how harshly he may be treated at work, he can come home to a safe place where he will be loved and appreciated? A Christian wife should ask her husband what specific areas he needs to have full confidence that he can entrust to her. Our son-in-law (Kathryn's husband) says that the only way he can leave home each day and concentrate on his work is that he has absolute confidence that his children are given the very best love and care possible.

Benefit #2

"She brings him good, and not harm, all the days of her life." This is not a self-centered woman, but neither is she a self-abasing woman. This woman fears the Lord, and her ethic is based on Biblical truth. She understands that her life-purpose is to glorify God. So the good she does is not based on whim or impulse. This is a clearly thought out determination to bring the goodness of God into her marriage. She may not always do what her husband wants, but she will do what he needs. She will neither indulge nor enable sinful behavior, for that would do him harm. She will lovingly encourage him to take the high road rather than to take the easy road. Which leads to the third benefit of a virtuous wife.

Benefit #3

"Her husband is respected at the city gate, where he takes his seat among the elders of the land." The city gate represents the place where the affairs of life were conducted. "The city gate was extremely important in the life of the people, for social, administrative, and business intercourse took place there. . . . Here kings as well as city elders sat to administer justice. . . . It was considered an honor to sit among the elders at the gate. . . . Legal transactions also took place here . . . and it served as a marketplace. . . ."[3] The partnership of a virtuous woman energizes a man to develop his potential and to assume a place of leadership in whatever arena of life God calls him to serve. Christian men who are supported by wives of noble character can permeate culture with confidence and boldness.

HER WORKS PRAISE HER

Lemuel's mother concludes with an interesting statement: "Give her the reward she has earned, and let her works bring her praise at the city gate."

The Christian wife's "work" will bring her praise at the city gate. What is going on at the city gate? Her husband is there. And whatever he is, whatever he does, reflects on her. If she has done her work of supporting him well, then she will be praised. Unfortunately, few women today see that their first and foremost responsibility and privilege is to glorify God by supporting their husband. But few women bought that idea in Lemuel's day. That is why his mother told him that such a woman was a rare jewel!

There is something here that should be mentioned. It is not the woman's children who will bring her praise at the city gate. Yet when she makes this supreme investment in her husband, "her children arise and call her blessed." I fear that too many women become so totally absorbed in their children that years go by with little energy aimed toward their husbands. When the children leave, two strangers remain with only a superficial relationship. We must guard against this tendency.

But isn't this risky? What about the Christian woman whose husband is an unbeliever, and he brings her grief rather than praise? Or what about the countless women who have invested their lives in their husbands, only to have them walk out after twenty years of marriage? What praise is there in that? These women's pain is beyond description. The Christian woman in this situation must remember that we do not live for men's praise but for God's glory. Her obedience may go unrecognized and unappreciated on earth, but she will be praised by her Father when He greets her at the gates of the Celestial City with that glorious welcome, "Well done, good and faithful servant. . . . Come and share your Master's happiness!" (Matthew 25:21).

Many say there is a crisis of male leadership in the Christian world today. If this is true, could it be that part of the reason is there are not enough women who are helping their husbands to fulfill their calling or exhorting their sons to seek out women of virtue?

Jeff Hudson has found a wife of noble character. Jeff was a computer programmer in a State office. When there were cutbacks, he was terminated. Then he was rehired as a clerk. When Jeff and Dena's son Brett was born, Dena left her teaching position to be a full-time mom. Becoming a one-income family was a scary thing to do, but for Jeff and Dena it was the right thing to do. Then Jeff was promoted to another computer position. But he soon realized that some of the contracts he was to work on were with Planned Parenthood clinics and other clinics with questionable criteria. "I sat there unable to touch those contracts," he said. "I knew I had to tell my boss, and I had to tell Dena." Dena did not flinch. "If necessary, I will go back to my teaching job," she assured him. Jeff's supervisor could offer only one option other than termination. Jeff was allowed to return to his former position and former pay.

Jeff is a man who can "sit at the city gate" of our culture and confront that culture head to head, toe to toe, because he has a wife who supports him. Their decision did not stop abortion. Realistically it probably did not prevent even one abortion. But they did make a difference in the battle "against the spiritual forces of evil in the heavenly realms" (Ephesians 6: 12).

They also made a difference in their testimony to their son. Dena shared with me, and with you, a very personal letter she wrote in Brett's baby book:

> Brett, your daddy did something recently that will be a great example to you. A few weeks ago he started a new job. It wasn't going to be much more money, but the position had room for advancement and Dad would be using computers (which he's good at) and dressing up (which makes you feel important). But he found out that much of the job involved dealing with issues that we as Christians cannot condone. Your Dad went to his new boss and explained his convictions. When he came home and told me that he might lose his job, I was scared. It was a very different feeling than when Dad was laid off. I was still teaching then. If he lost this job, it would cut our income to $0! I knew God would be there for us, but it would take nothing short of a miracle for us to make it. I told your Dad that we could both start looking for a job and whoever got an offer first would take it, though it would have killed me to leave you if I had been the 'lucky' one. I think Dad was scared too, Brett. He takes his role as a provider very seriously, and I think he thought I would get hysterical and panic. Now, here's my example to you son. I am a Christian first, a wife second, and a mother third. I knew God was in control, and I knew I had to stand by your Dad no matter what. I take my marriage vows very seriously and loss of a job does not constitute petty whining or divorce. I am with your Dad "till death do us part." If you read no other page in this book, please read this one. When you grow up, you want to be strong in your convictions, and you want to look for a godly wife who will back you up. Our reward is in heaven.

Jeff has what Lemuel's mother desired for her son. And little Brett has a mother who is encouraging him to act kingly and to pursue noble goals.

A BIBLICAL MODEL

King Xerxes also found a wife of noble character, though he probably never fully realized nor appreciated his treasure.

When the search was on to find "beautiful young virgins for the king" (Esther 2:2) so that he could select one to be queen, a young Jewish girl named Esther was ultimately chosen. This stunning story of courage and obedience captures the heart of every Christian woman. But Esther was much more than a pretty face in the right place at the right time to achieve fame. Esther was a woman who feared the Lord. Her decision to go before the king and plead for her people catapulted her to the status of heroine. But Esther had already displayed her true colors by protecting and supporting her husband.

King Xerxes was not the husband of every girl's dreams. He had a drinking problem, he disposed of his first wife because she displeased him, and to say that he was self-centered is an understatement. But God sovereignly placed Esther in this position, and she humbly accepted her assignment.

Shortly after Esther became queen, her cousin Mordecai informed her of a plot to assassinate the king (Esther 2:19-23). Esther could have kept quiet and been rid of this arrogant, insensitive man—her husband. But Esther did the right thing. She informed him of the plot and saved his life. His callous indifference is obvious in the fact that he did not even acknowledge his gratitude to Esther nor to Mordecai. But the event was recorded in the book of the annals.

Esther's ethic was based on the character and promises of Jehovah. For her, the issue was not expediency but obedience. For some reason, God had placed her in the palace of a heathen king. That reason eventually became clear when wicked Haman persuaded the king to issue an edict allowing the extermination of the Jews. The fact that Esther had done her husband "good and not harm" positioned her to go before him and plead for the life of her people.

The very night before she laid her request before her husband, he was unable to sleep. He instructed his attendant to read to him from the book of the annals. The attendant randomly opened the book, but God sovereignly guided the pages. And at a strategic moment Xerxes was reminded of the good his wife and Mordecai

had done for him. Esther's request was granted. God's people
were spared.

Esther was a heroine to her people and a helper to her husband. She protected and supported her husband even though it
must have been a difficult marriage. I know that this raises some
tough questions. And there are no easy answers. But a letter to
Dr. James Dobson, and his answer, give a marvelous story and
some practical advice.

A HELPER SUPPORTER

A woman wrote: "I agree with your belief that the father should
be the spiritual leader in the family, but it just doesn't happen
that way at our house. If the kids go to church on Sunday, it's
because I wake them up and see that they get ready. If we have
family devotions, it's done at my insistence, and I'm the one who
prays with the children at bedtime. If I didn't do these things, our
kids would have no spiritual training. Nevertheless, people keep
saying I should wait for my husband to accept spiritual leadership
in our family. What do you advise?"

Dr. Dobson answered:

That's an extremely important question and a subject of controversy
right now. As you indicated, some Christian leaders instruct women
to wait passively for their husbands to assume spiritual responsibility. Until that leadership is accepted, they recommend that wives
stay out of the way and let God put pressure on the husband to
assume the role He's given to men.

I strongly disagree with that view when small children are involved.
If the issue focused only on the spiritual welfare of a husband and
wife, then a woman could afford to bide her time. However, the
presence of boys and girls changes the picture dramatically. Every
day that goes by without spiritual training for them is a day that can
never be recaptured.

Therefore, if your husband is not going to accept the role of spiritual
leadership that God has given him, then I believe *you* must do it.
You have no time to lose. You should continue taking the family to

church on Sunday. You should pray with the children and teach them to read the Bible. Furthermore, you must continue your private devotions and maintain your own relationship with God.

In short, I feel that the spiritual life of children (and adults) is simply too important for a woman to postpone for two or four or six years, hoping her husband will eventually awaken. Jesus made it clear that members of our own family can erect the greatest barriers to our faith, but they must not be permitted to do so. He says, "Do not suppose that I have come to bring peace on earth. I have not come to bring peace, but a sword. For I have come to turn a man against his father, a daughter against her mother, a daughter-in-law against her mother-in-law—a man's enemies will be the members of his own household. Anyone who loves his father or mother more than me is not worthy of me; [and] anyone who loves son or daughter more than me is not worthy of me" (Matt. 10:34-37).

I remember my grandfather R. L. Dobson. He was a moral man who saw no need for the Christian faith. His spiritual disinterest placed my grandmother, Juanita Dobson, under great pressure, for she was a devout Christian who felt she must put God first. Therefore, she accepted the responsibility of introducing her six children to Jesus Christ. There were times when my grandfather exerted tremendous pressure on her, not to give up her faith, but to leave him out of it.

He said, "I am a good father and provider, I pay my bills, and I am honest in dealing with my fellow man. That is enough."

His wife replied, "You are a good man, but that is *not* enough. You should give your heart to God." This he could not comprehend.

My 97-pound grandmother made no attempt to force her faith on her husband, nor did she treat him disrespectfully. But she quietly continued to pray and fast for the man she loved. For more than 40 years she brought this same petition before God on her knees.

Then, at 69 years of age, my grandfather suffered a stroke, and for the first time in his life he was desperately ill. One day his daughter came into his room to clean and straighten. As she walked by his bed, she saw tears in his eyes. No one had ever seen him cry before.

"Daddy, what's wrong?" she asked.

He responded, "Honey, go to the head of the stairs and call your mother."

My grandmother ran to her husband's side and heard him say, "I know I'm going to die, and I'm not afraid of death, but it's so dark. There's no way out. I've lived my whole life through and missed the one thing that really matters. Will you pray for me?"

"Will I pray?" exclaimed my grandmother. She had been hoping for that request throughout her adult life. She fell to her knees, and the intercessions of 40 years seemed to pour out through that bedside prayer. R. L. Dobson gave his heart to God that day in a wonderful way.

During the next two weeks, he asked to see some of the church people whom he had offended and requested their forgiveness. He concluded his personal affairs, and then he died with a testimony on his lips. Before descending into a coma from which he would never awaken, my grandfather said, ". . . Now there is a way through the darkness."

The unrelenting prayers of my little grandmother had been answered.

Returning to the question, I would like to caution women not to become "self-righteous" and critical of their husbands. Let everything be done in a spirit of love. However, there may be some lonely years when the burden of spiritual leadership with children must be carried alone. If that is the case, the Lord has promised to walk with you through these difficult days.[4]

Juanita Dobson placed the helper signature firmly upon the soul of her family history. And the voices calling her blessed continue to the third generation.

ANN HAMILTON

The dates of Ann Hamilton's sojourn on earth were approximately 1750 to 1800. Her legacy of faith is inscribed on the hearts of her descendants to the seventh generation.

She was known in her Scottish village as a devout Christian whose countenance radiated the peace of her Lord. The story has been handed down from generation to generation that on her deathbed, her family observed that her sweet countenance changed to one of worry and anxiety. Perplexed, they asked what was wrong. She was finally able to give them an answer, and when she did her expression changed once more to radiance. "Children," she said, "I have it. He has given me the promise." And she quoted Isaiah 59:21:

> As for me, this is my covenant with them, saith the Lord; My Spirit, that is upon thee, and my words which I have put in thy mouth, shall not depart out of thy mouth, nor out of the mouth of thy seed, nor out of the mouth of thy seed's seed, saith the Lord, from henceforth and for ever. (KJV)

She was claiming that covenant promise for the future, and God has honored His promise to that Scottish mother.

Among her fifth generation descendants are John Armes, Willard Armes, Katherine Armes Holliday, and Janet Armes Ludlam. The men were Presbyterian ministers, and the women, wives of ministers. All of their children are committed Christians, some serving as pastors, missionaries, heads of Christian schools, deacons, elders, chaplains. One had strayed from the faith, only to be convicted upon hearing of Ann Hamilton's story. Today he is in the ministry.

The story has been shared at family baptisms and funerals—most recently at services for John, who had retired after serving for many years as a missionary in Africa. In that service, the entire family stood together and recited Isaiah 59:21.

The covenant verse was engraved on a silver plaque many years ago that was passed on to Willard, and duplicates now hang in the homes of most living descendants. Wherever and however it is told or read, it is a powerful testimony of God's covenant promises.

There are now sixty-one grandchildren who are hearing the story from their parents, continuing the covenantal chain claimed by Ann Hamilton so many years ago.[1]

Chapter 8

HELPER-PROTECTOR

We wait in hope for the Lord; He is our help and our shield.
(Psalm 33:20)

A shield is an article of protective armor, a means of defense. One who shields another acts or serves as a protector, defender, or safeguard.

Psalm 33 was apparently composed at some time when God intervened and delivered the nation of Israel from oppression. It is a call to the righteous to praise the Ruler of the world for being the Defender of His people:

> Sing joyfully to the Lord, you righteous;
> > it is fitting for the upright to praise him. (verse 1)

The Psalmist then gives reasons why it is fitting for the righteous to praise the Lord:

> For the word of the Lord is right and true;
> > he is faithful in all he does.
> The Lord loves righteousness and justice;
> > the earth is full of his unfailing love.
>
> By the word of the Lord were the heavens made,
> > their starry host by the breath of his mouth.
> He gathers the waters of the sea into jars;
> > he puts the deep into storehouses . . .
>
> The Lord foils the plans of the nations;
> > he thwarts the purposes of the peoples.
> But the plans of the Lord stand firm forever.
> > the purposes of his heart through all generations.
> > (verses 4–11)

God's justice, goodness, truth, and love, His power seen in creation, His sovereignty over the governments of the world, should make us sing joyfully to Him. But the crescendo of this praise comes as the Psalmist speaks of the special favor God shows to his own chosen people and of His protection over His children who hope in Him:

> From heaven the Lord looks down
> and sees all mankind;
> from his dwelling place he watches
> all who live on earth—
> he who forms the hearts of all,
> who considers everything they do.
> No king is saved by the size of his army;
> no warrior escapes by his great strength.
> A horse is a vain hope for deliverance;
> despite all its great strength it cannot save.
>
> But the eyes of the Lord are on those who fear him,
> on those whose hope is in his unfailing love,
> to deliver them from death
> and keep them alive in famine. (verses 13–19)

No wonder the Psalmist erupts into another serenade of praise:

> We wait in hope for the Lord;
> he is our help and our shield.
> In him our hearts rejoice,
> for we trust in his holy name.
> May your unfailing love rest upon us, O Lord.
> even as we put our hope in you. (verses 20–22)

The Lord God knows the frailty of His children, and He is a help and shield to them. He is " . . . a help to furnish them with and forward them in that which is good, and a shield to fortify them against and protect them from every thing that is evil."[2]

Often when God speaks of shielding His children He uses the imagery of a mother:

> O Jerusalem, Jerusalem, you who kill the prophets and stone those sent to you, how often I have longed to gather your children together, as a hen gathers her chicks under her wings, but you were not willing. (Matthew 23:37)

> As a mother comforts her child, so will I comfort you. (Isaiah 66:13)

A MOTHER'S HEART

In I Kings 3 we read of two women who came to Solomon with a problem:

> Now two prostitutes came to the king and stood before him. One of them said, "My lord, this woman and I live in the same house. I had a baby while she was there with me. The third day after my child was born, the woman also had a baby. We were alone; there was no one in the house but the two of us.

> "During the night this woman's son died because she lay on him. So she got up in the middle of the night and took my son from my side while I your servant was asleep. She put him by her breast and put her dead son by my breast. The next morning, I got up to nurse my son—and he was dead! But when I looked at him closely in the morning light, I saw that it wasn't the son I had borne."

> The other woman said, "No! The dead one is yours; the living one is mine." And so they argued before the king.

In Solomon's court, this dispute did not require a long, drawn-out court battle. It was settled in record time!

> Then the king said, "Bring me a sword." So they brought a sword for the king. He then gave an order: "Cut the living child in two and give half to one and half to the other."

> The woman whose son was alive was filled with compassion for her son and said to the king, "Please, my lord, give her the living baby! Don't kill him!"

> But the other said, "Neither I nor you shall have him. Cut him in two!"

> Then the king gave his ruling: "Give the living baby to the first woman. Do not kill him; she is his mother."

> When all Israel heard the verdict the king had given, they held the king in awe, because they saw that he had wisdom from God to administer justice. (I Kings 3:16–28)

Solomon knew that a mother's heart will cause her to protect her child regardless of the consequences or sacrifices. It is the nature of a mother to shield and protect her children, but we do not have to give birth to activate this nature. It is part of our female design. It is activated in those who desire to reflect the character of their Heavenly Father. They desire to furnish children with and "forward them in that which is good, and to fortify them against and protect them from every thing that is evil."

So this chapter is not just about mothers. It is about all women who have a mother's heart. It takes faith and fortitude to activate this aspect of our female design because the task is great and the environment is hostile. And motherhood is under attack.

In *Children At Risk,* Dr. James Dobson and Gary Bauer, write:

> The vanguard of the attack against mothers was led by the troops of the feminist movement in the '60s and '70s. Militant feminists argued that the job of caring for children was a form of oppression, slavery, or imprisonment. Some feminists compared the mental state of homemakers to soldiers in World War II who had suffered severe emotional damage in combat.

> In 1970, Germaine Greer wrote *The Female Eunuch* which condemned motherhood as a handicap and pregnancy as an illness. Greer urged women to be "deliberately promiscuous" and to be certain not to conceive children. Broadening her attack against the whole institution of marriage, she concluded, "If women are to effect a significant amelioration in their condition, it seems obvious that they must refuse to marry."

> The classic critique on motherhood and family was Betty Friedan's, *The Feminine Mystique.* Friedan described the family as an oppressive institution. She compared homemakers to "parasites" and said that sexist ideas were "burying millions of American women alive."

Not surprisingly, this anti-mother/anti-family rhetoric disgusted millions of American women, including many who were sympathetic to some feminist goals. The rejection of motherhood helped to derail the movement as a political force in the '80s. But today, the hostility to motherhood is no longer limited to the feminist fringe. Like so many other attacks on traditional institutions, this one has been embraced by the cultural elites and has become their established worldview.[3]

Many children are going up against the enemies of secularism, humanism, materialism, relativism, and subjectivism with no shield. Theodore Roosevelt said, "If the mother does not do her duty, there will either be no next generation, or a next generation that is worse than none at all."[4]

Are we approaching that time? We are perilously close unless we women with a mother's heart do our duty.

But what is our duty? As always, we can look to God's Word for Biblical models.

A MOTHER IN ISRAEL

When the Israelites entered the Promised Land, they were told to rid the land of the Canaanites, but after the death of Joshua they were content to co-exist with them. In time co-existence changed to intermingling and intermarrying. As always happens when the Church conforms rather than transforms, evil overcame good, sin overcame righteousness, and unbelief overcame faith.

Israel broke the covenant, but God's faithfulness persisted. He allowed them to be oppressed by their enemies so they would turn to Him, and when they did, He sent judges who held up God's covenant promises and conditions before the people and who shielded them against their enemies.

One of those judges was a woman. "Deborah, a prophetess, the wife of Lappidoth, was leading Israel at that time. She held court under the Palm of Deborah between Ramah and Bethel in the hill country of Ephraim, and the Israelites came to her to have their disputes decided" (Judges 4:4-5).

Israel had been oppressed by Jabin, a king of Canaan, for twenty years. The people called out to the Lord for help.

Deborah summoned Barak and said, "The Lord, the God of Israel, commands you: 'Go, take with you ten thousand men . . . and lead the way to Mount Tabor. I will lure Sisera, the commander of Jabin's army, with his chariots and his troops . . . and give him into your hands' " (Judges 4:7).

After God gave this deliverance, Deborah penned and sang a song of praise to the Lord. I am attracted to this entire story, but there are three verses in Deborah's song that I am drawn to like a magnet:

> Village life in Israel ceased,
>   ceased until I, Deborah arose,
>   arose a mother in Israel.
> When they chose new gods,
>   war came to the city gates,
> and not a shield or spear was seen
>   among forty thousand in Israel.
> My heart is with Israel's princes,
>   with the willing volunteers among the people.
>   Praise the Lord! (Judges 5:7-9)

There was no sense of community, no reverence for God, and no protectors until God raised up "a mother in Israel." Deborah's mother's heart was with Israel's princes, and this inspired them to action. Her passion for God lit a fire in Israel that resulted in peace for forty years.

There is no mention of Deborah being a biological mother, but she was a woman of courage, vision, and action. She chose to describe herself as a "mother in Israel."

We live in a time of unbelief, oppression, and apathy. There is no village life in our culture and often there is no village life in the Church. There is a need for "mothers in Israel" to defy culture and to restore community to the Church and family. And Deborah shows us that this is the opportunity of all women with a mother's heart.

A MOTHER IN THE HOME

When Paul wrote to young Timothy he said, "I long to see you, so that I may be filled with joy. I have been reminded of your sincere faith, which first lived in your grandmother Lois and in your mother Eunice and, I am persuaded, now lives in you also" (II Timothy 1:5).

Later Paul said to Timothy, "But as for you, continue in what you have learned and have become convinced of, because you know those from whom you learned it, and how from infancy you have known the holy Scriptures, which are able to make you wise for salvation through faith in Christ Jesus" (II Timothy 3:15-15).

The image of this grandmother and mother nurturing little Timothy is very special to me. My mother is still involved in the nurturing of our adult children, and now we both have the joy of loving my grandchildren. We, like Lois and Eunice, believe in the Biblical theme of grace running in lines of generations. We cling to God's promise to Abraham: "I will establish my covenant as an everlasting covenant between me and you and your descendants after you for the generations to come, to be your God *and the God of your descendants after you*" (Genesis 17:7, emphasis mine). This promise was repeated by Peter at Pentecost: "Repent and be baptized, every one of you, in the name of Jesus Christ so that your sins may be forgiven. And you will receive the gift of the Holy Spirit. The promise is for you *and your children* and for all who are far off—for all whom the Lord our God will call" (Acts 2:38–39, emphasis mine).

Lois and Eunice must have been women with a multi-generational vision who were committed to "tell the next generation the praiseworthy deeds of the Lord, his power, and the wonders he has done . . . so the next generation would know them, even the children yet to be born, and they in turn would tell their children. Then they would put their trust in God and would not forget his deeds but would keep his commands" (Psalm 78:4, 6-7).

I have the distinct feeling that they claimed the words of the Psalmists for young Timothy:

> You brought me out of the womb;
>> you made me trust in you even at my mother's breast.
> From birth I was cast upon you;
>> from my mother's womb you have been my God.
>> (Psalm 22:9-10)

> For you have been my hope, O Sovereign Lord,
>> my confidence since my youth.
> From birth I have relied on you;
>> you brought me forth from my mother's womb.
> I will ever praise you. (Psalm 71:5-6)

Lois and Eunice had an agenda for Timothy. Power and prominence in the world were not part of that agenda. They protected him against the moral decay of their day by saturating him with Scripture from infancy. And the result was that Timothy was a key figure in advancing the Kingdom of Jesus Christ.

ROCKING OUR WORLD

"The hand that rocks the cradle rules the world"[5] clearly states the influence of women. We could capture culture for Christ in the next generation if Christian women, whether mothers in Israel or mothers in the home, would train our children to live as Kingdom people.

Kay Coles James held several positions of power in the Bush administration. She is a Christian with a bold and uncompromising testimony for the Lord. In her book *Never Forget,* Kay writes about growing up in the days of segregation in the public housing projects in Richmond, Virginia. She tells about the sense of community among blacks when she was a child:

> Mama's teaching about honesty and hard work helped define us as individuals. We knew who we were. It was also about this time that I developed a sense of pride in my people. . . . Segregation also gave rise to unimaginable acts of solidarity and kindness within the black community. When you couldn't make your rent because you had lost your job or had a medical emergency, you threw a "rent party." . . . Friday night you'd cook a bunch of food and have some drinks

on hand to sell; everyone would come to your place and sit around and talk, and by the end of two days you'd have enough money pay your rent. . . . We survived because we depended on one another. . . . We also got along because we helped each other. . . .

Who were the people who taught me to think for myself and speak out my convictions? Who were the people who taught me to diagram sentences, memorize Psalm 23, and hold my head up high? They were teachers like Mrs. Hembry, Mrs. Mitchell, Mr. Kemp, and Mrs. Hubbard. They were people like Mrs. Watkins in the office. Much of the transformation can be attributed to people like Elsie Lewis, the principal of Webster Davis. . . .

At Webster Davis you never heard children complaining to their teachers that such-and-such was not fair. We knew that such objections would get us nowhere. "Life is not fair" I heard many a teacher snap, "and so don't go looking for fair." We accepted the inherent difficulties and injustices of life as we accepted the stifling humidity of Richmond summers. We didn't like it, and we stiffened our resolve to fight against it, but we conditioned ourselves to persevere and thrive in spite of it. And we knew with a knowing so deep that they must have seasoned the water fountains with it, that life was going to be tough. We never expected it to be easy. No one at Webster Davis, or in the black community at large, ever led us to believe that we could expect to get anything in life that we didn't sweat, bleed, and work for.

But even as our teachers painted us a realistic picture of black life in the fifties, they held up examples of those who had gone before us who had triumphed when the world was even more unfair. . . . Their realism didn't discourage us. It encouraged us to succeed and flourish and overcome.[6]

We need to infuse this sense of community and identity in the children in our churches. Our children need to understand that Christians are a minority, and they must learn to think Biblically and speak out their convictions. Rather than social skills, sports, popularity, designer clothes, and so forth, having top priority, we need to shape our children into Kingdom people. Christianization should supersede socialization. We need to instill in our children a vision for going into culture with a Biblical worldview. But for them to go up against the materialism and relativism of our day, for them to survive and thrive as Christians in a pluralistic culture, we must teach them to integrate their faith into all of life. We must condition them "to persevere and thrive in spite of" a hostile culture. We must give them a vision to "succeed and flourish and overcome" for the honor and glory of our King. Our children are Kingdom people. They are not to be shaped by culture; they are to be shapers of culture.

Pastor Robert S. Rayburn explains that it is the phenomenon of covenant succession (Christian parents producing a godly seed) that has furnished the Church with:

> generation after generation of great multitudes of Christian servants and soldiers who reach manhood and womanhood well taught, sturdy in faith, animated by love for God and man, sophisticated in the ways of the world and the Devil, polished in the manners of genuine Christian brotherhood, overshadowed by the specter of the Last Day, nerved to deny themselves and take up their cross so as to be counted worthy of greater exploits for Christ and Kingdom. Presently the church not only suffers a terrible shortage of such otherworldly and resolute Christians, superbly prepared for spiritual warfare, but, in fact, is hemorrhaging its children into the world. Christian evangelism will never make a decisive difference in our culture when it amounts merely to an effort to replace losses due to widespread desertion from our own camp. The gospel will always fail to command attention and carry conviction when large numbers of those who grow up under its influence are observed abandoning it for the world . . . inscribing the doctrine of covenant succession upon the heart of family and church must have a wonderfully solemnizing and galvanizing effect. It will set Christian parents seriously to work on the spiritual nurture of their children, equipping them and requiring them to live the life of covenant faith and duty to which their God and Savior called them at the headwaters of life. And, ever conscious of the greater effect of parental example, they will forsake the easy way, shamelessly and joyfully to live a life of devotion and obedience which adorns and ennobles the faith in the eyes of their children.[7]

Women could rock our world by rocking our babies!

A HELPER-DEFENDER

Connie Farquhar is rocking her world in Northeast, Maryland. To say that Connie has a mother's heart is a colossal understatement! Few can do what Connie and her husband are doing, but we can be stretched by their example to protect the children. This story is told in Connie's own words:

> When I first received the letter asking me to write about our family ministry, I knew that we had once again been misunderstood. You see, we don't have a ministry, but rather are the recipients of God's special ministry to shape and fine tune His children. God has chosen to use my children and their circumstances to make my husband and me able to be used by Him. The Lord has blessed us with eleven children, eight born within our hearts and three born of our bodies.

> Thirteen years ago, after being blessed with a beautiful baby girl and becoming totally enthralled in the frills and ruffles, I had opened the door for discipline through my own sinful pride. I was so proud of my offspring. And if one little girl wasn't enough for any mother's ego, I was soon blessed with another.

> Soon afterwards, a little boy was born. He was strong, handsome and very healthy. But my next pregnancy was very complicated and ended in the death of our little one. I was unable to conceive more children, but my husband and I both felt that God intended us to have a larger family. He had graciously provided us with a big house and plenty of room for children to play. We heard about some Christian families who were foster parents, and we decided we would care for these needy children until we could find a normal baby to adopt. And this is when God really started to change our hearts.

> Our first placement occurred in the middle of a snowstorm. The agency called saying they had a drug-addicted baby that no one would take. So I packed my three children up and plowed through the snow in our little car. When we first saw him, my heart sank. He was barely four pounds, not a strand of hair on his head, and there were tubes and wires coming out of everywhere on his little body. He lay shaking in the bed, which the nurse explained was due to withdrawal from the drugs he was exposed to in utero and the hefty

sedative his mother had given him days before to try and settle his constant crying. For the first seven months of his life, my husband and I would take turns sleeping next to the cradle with one hand on his chest and one ear listening to his monitor. He suffered through DTs longer than any alcoholic I had ever seen. One year after his birth, the social worker called and said that his mother had asked if we would adopt him. We were in such shock. We had come to love this little one and learned so much from his fragile condition. So just before Mother's Day, Brenton Matthew Farquhar became our second son.

We continued to foster and saw 27 children through our home. Still we had hopes for adopting a healthy, normal baby. One day a call came about three siblings who had been placed in another foster home, which could no longer care for them because of their constant fighting and poor behavior. We agreed to take them and went to pick them up. Again my sinful heart saw three of the homeliest children I had ever seen. The two-week-old baby was very sick and they all had "creepy crawlers" everywhere. The children had been neglected so severely that their little minds had never grown.

Three long years later, our new additions became Farquhars. These emotionally disturbed children were a totally new horizon, and one which God had sent to work on my sin of impatience. We felt our family might be complete at this point, but I should have known that I still had some real problem areas which another child could help. You see, all seven of our children up to this point looked basically normal. Their behavior, medical, and developmental problems were easy to hide. I tend to be an overly sensitive person and never wanted a child who would make us stand out or cause people to stare. I felt so sorry for families with handicapped children. How sad their lives must be.

So in God's wonderful sovereignty, He sent us Sharrah. She was born also with cocaine addiction and had been given up at birth. She had never been placed for adoption because the doctors felt she could only live a few months. The drugs and complications had left Sharrah with renal disease, blindness, severe cerebral palsy, brain damage and an inability to eat on her own. She was literally dying of malnutrition.

I didn't relish the prospect of a terminal child, but I knew that if God would bring her into our lives that He would also bring us through her death. Our Sharrah Melissa was a powerful blessing in our lives. We were told over and over by doctors that she offered no productivity by staying alive, and it would be better to let her waste away. This child whom God chose to live on this earth had all the value she ever needed because she was created by a loving Father. She served her Lord well, by ministering to us and countless others. She forced me to give a reason for the hope that is within me and to know that life is precious because of Who created it at the beginning . . . not what it has accomplished in worldly terms at the end.

As handicapped as Sharrah was, she still looked fairly normal. She was God's way of easing us into our next child. Brocton had spent several years of his life in an institution where they were doing the bare minimum until he died. As a toddler he had been so severely abused that he was left comatose and burned on 80 percent of his body. For a moment I questioned why God had allowed him to live. You see what a slow learner I am! I was so angry at the persons who had left him so close to death, and how God must be angry at their loathsome sins. As my righteous indignation flourished, God rebuked me. The anger that had led to Broc's abuse was just like the anger with which I so often struggled. And the disappointment that God felt was the same He felt toward my sin. Broc really taught me humility. I was not better than the people who abused him apart from the fact that my sins had been paid for by a wonderful Savior.

June 1992 brought God's gift of a severely disabled infant who rapidly became Bronson Timothy to us. When we went to Orlando, Florida, for his adoption, our van exploded. But God furnished a replacement through the International Rotary Convention that was being held in Orlando that very week!

Nine months later, Broc, then five and a half, died with Mom and Dad and all nine of his siblings holding his little hands. We struggled with questions of God's timing until fifteen weeks later our three and a half year old little princess died in her crib early one morning after an hour of unsuccessful CPR by Mom and Dad. God's timing was for our support. He had gently led us into the valley of parenting terminal children.

Miraculously, as only he can, a six-month-old little girl arrived in our home from Russia just two weeks before Sharrah's death. Sacha Brianna is truly God's gift given to make bearable the tremendous pain in a mother's arms and father's eyes when the Lord takes their children home.

We still get many stares and many questions. Our family loves to eat out and go window shopping through the mall. We also have been blessed with the experience of home schooling seven of our children. Each of these areas has opened so many doors for evangelism and given us many valuable experiences. We are always asked if our family is now finished. My husband usually replies that his quiver is comfortable but maybe not full. For several years, my family has shared the prayer to adopt an HIV child, and if that fits into God's plan perhaps that will be next. In the meantime, we look forward to the new lessons that God has for us and are so thankful that as sinners we are saved by grace. We are also very thankful for the gentle discipline and teaching which God has administered to us through our eleven children.

MOTHERING MOMENTS

Again, we are not all called or equipped to do what Connie and her husband are doing in the battle for the hearts of our children. But we can do something. Dobson and Bauer state: "To our way of thinking, *women* are the key to this contest. Whether at home or in the work force, many of them have seen firsthand the effects of our flight from family and faith. What an incredible army these millions of mothers could be, most of whom believe in responsible living, in traditional standards of right and wrong, and in the God of our fathers."[8]

What can we do to join that army even if we are not in the mothering stage of life? There are Christian education books that go into great depth about the Church's responsibility, and parenting books to help parents in each stage of the parenting process. But I want to consider some ordinary things that each of us can do to protect the children. I want to think about things we can do that require minimum time but can have significant results. I call them "Mothering Moments," and this is what they look like.

- A widow invites some teenage girls from church to come to her home for tea. She gets to know them and tells them how important they are in the church family.

- A Sunday School teacher cultivates a servant heart in her class of ten-year-old boys and girls by taking them to her home to bake cookies for shut-ins. Then they deliver the cookies and sing hymns for their elderly friends.

- Each woman in a women's Bible study group takes the name of a child or youth in the church and commits to pray daily for that child. She periodically writes notes of encouragement to the child, or calls and asks for prayer requests.

- A woman offers to teach a child how to knit, and as they build a friendship she encourages obedient living.

- A Christian teacher in the public school system prays for her class each day and lives before them an example of love and justice.

- An empty-nester develops a friendship with several girls in the church and takes them on special outings. She often includes children from other countries whose fathers are working in the area, or children from a homeless shelter. She teaches the children to show the love of Jesus by building bridges of friendship to people of other cultures, races, and socio-economic groups.

- A single woman spends time with teenage girls and talks with them about sexual purity. She promises to pray for them, and tells them to call her whenever they are struggling with compromising their standards.

- A woman with no children offers to help a mother who is home schooling.

- A team of women from a church go regularly to the shelter for battered women and read to the children. Another team works in the crisis pregnancy counseling center. Another goes to the hospital to help care for AIDS babies.

- A woman writes Scripture promises on cards and gives them to children at church. She hugs the child and says, "You are a Kingdom child, and here is a promise from our King."

- A woman invites a young widow or divorcee and her children to celebrate a holiday with her family.

- A grandmother takes her grandchild to play with a mentally or physically handicapped child so that the children will learn how to learn from and minister to each other. She also suggests that the mother of the handicapped child use this time to run errands or go for a walk in the park.

- A woman praises a child's art work, or musical ability, or rock collection, or interest in computers, or love for science and says, "God has given you this interest. It will be exciting to see how He will use you to be salt and light in the world for Him."

- A woman approaches the manager of a supermarket and gently expresses her concern about the magazines displayed at the checkout counter. "The covers of these magazines are sending messages to our young girls that being skinny and beautiful is the ultimate goal of life. Would you consider putting wrappers on the provocative covers, or moving them to a different location?"

- A woman invites several children to her home one afternoon a week, and she reads them stories of Christian heroes.

- A Sunday School teacher looks at each child in her class and realizes afresh that she may be teaching a future United States president, school teacher, minister, concert pianist, president of a corporation, elder in a church, mom, dad, missionary, mechanic, Sunday School teacher, nurse, office manager, etc. She visualizes them taking the love of Jesus into each of those segments of life and she prepares them for the task.

Mothering Moments are a compelling way to rock our world. We are an "incredible army" with a powerful potential!

My heart rejoices in those parents and churches who are training their children for Kingdom living. They are keenly aware of the results of intermingling and intermarrying. They have heeded God's warning not to be ensnared by the worship of other gods: "You must not worship the Lord your God in their way. . . . They even burn their sons and daughters in the fire as sacrifices to their gods" (Deuteronomy 12:31). They know that if we attempt to syncretize Biblical truth with current trends, we offer our sons and daughters on the altar to the gods of this world. And they know that the result will be that "Your sons and daughters will be given to another nation, and you will wear out your eyes watching for them day after day, powerless to lift a hand" (Deuteronomy 28:32).

These parents and churches cling to the rich promises of God. They hold before their children the noble goals that Lemuel's mother held before him: "Speak up for those who cannot speak for themselves, for the rights of all who are destitute. Speak up and judge fairly; defend the rights of the poor and needy" (Proverbs 31:8-9).

They have seized the truth of Scripture and are training up a generation of Kingdom people who will not only infiltrate culture, but will populate heaven. They are the protectors of the children:

> All your sons will be taught by the Lord,
>   and great will be your children's peace. (Isaiah 54:13)

ELIZABETH FRY

Elizabeth Fry was seventeen when she heard a sermon and was convicted that *God is.* Apparently the outward expression of this inner conviction was obvious, for five months later an older woman told her that she should be "a light to the blind, speech to the dumb, and feet to the lame." The course for her life was set. An entry in her journal reveals her determination not to lose her bearings:

> "I feel by experience how much entering into the world hurts me; it leads me to the love of pomp and vanity, to jealousy and ambition. . . . I love to feel for the sorrows of others. I love to pour wine and oil into the wounds of the afflicted. . . . I must use extreme exertion to act really right, to avoid idleness and dissipation."

The growth of these convictions into steady piety was slow, and the struggles she went through with temptations within and without were many and long, struggles with pride and vanity and idleness.

But always the desire to serve her Lord remained predominant, to serve Him by succoring all around her, and more especially the ignorant, and needy, and lost.

She gathered the poor children near her father's house into a large laundry and taught them daily.

She went into an asylum for the insane to comfort a poor woman she had known, whose reason had given way.

Two years after this beginning of a new life, in 1800, when nineteen years of age, Elizabeth married Mr. Fry.

She bore him eleven children.

It was not until 1812, twelve years after her marriage, that the characteristic charitable work of her life, the visiting and succoring female criminals in prison, by which she is known throughout Christendom, began.

But throughout these twelve years she was practically learning more of the Christian faith, and of that humility as to herself in which she said all true religion has its root. And she was faithfully using every opportunity of serving and succoring all she could. . . .

Meantime, she delighted in her garden, and made her home bright for her children, taught them, prayed with them, took walks in the woods and fields with them, and nourished in them the healthy pleasure she had herself in flowers and shells, and in all this beautiful world.

Yet, through all these blessings, and this fullness of life, a constant sense of her own weaknesses and deficiencies kept her humble and dependent on the Saviour, her "Holy Helper," as she loved to call Him. She thought others much better than herself, and a deep yearning was in her heart to render larger services for Christ's sake to the needy, sinful world He had redeemed.

And at last the long-waited-for opening to such service came.

In February, 1813, Mrs. Fry was asked by a friend to visit the women's side of the great prison of Newgate, to see if anything could be done to alleviate the misery and to amend the moral condition of the wretched beings shut up there. . . .

Three hundred women, with their young children, were shut up together in four rooms, without sufficient clothing, absolutely without any beds but the floor, in the cold winter, with no one to guide or control them, and with nothing to do. They were allowed to receive money, and to buy as much intoxicating drink as they liked in the prison.

The result was that those four rooms were like dens of wild beasts. . . . The governor of the prison dreaded to approach their cells.

Into this den of iniquity Elizabeth Fry and her friend, Anna Buxton, fearlessly ventured; or, I should rather say, she ventured with a divine courage of pity which overcame her natural timidity.

Her dove-like face and majestic, matronly presence, her tender, gentle voice, so deep and sweet . . . made a calm in the clamor of oaths and quarreling.

The two Christian women knelt down and prayed.

"I heard weeping," Mrs. Fry said, in describing it. "A very solemn quiet was observed. It was a very striking scene; the poor people on their knees around us, in their deplorable condition."

That was the beginning of the work of the thirty remaining years of her life, a work which inspired and guided the amelioration of the prisons for women throughout Christendom.

Mrs. Fry went back to her home with a glow of pity in her heart for those wretched creatures. . . . She began with making woolen garments for them in her own house.

Four years later she organized an association of ladies to work with her. Their first project was a school for the children. Soon some of the mothers asked to join the classes, and order began to replace the chaos. Their next endeavor was a plan for employing the women.

The men in authority discouraged them. They said the prisoners would rebel, and any materials for work given them would be stolen.

Mrs. Fry only asked to be allowed to try. To this the authorities consented. Then the ladies called the women together, and frankly told them they could not be treated as children; if they were to be helped, they must enter into the plan heartily themselves.

One by one the different rules were proposed to them. There was to be a matron to superintend. The women were to be employed in needlework . . . or any other suitable employment. There was to be no begging, swearing, card-playing, quarreling, or immoral conversation. All bad books were to be excluded. The most orderly among themselves were to be set over them as monitors. They were to come with clean hands and faces to their work, and be quiet while at work. Every morning and evening they were to be collected by the ringing of a bell to hear the Holy Scriptures read.

As each separate rule was read the women held up their hands in token of consent.

In a few weeks the magistrates came again, and saw the results of the effort. The poor women were sitting quietly at work, and listening to reading, decently dressed, with calm and cheerful faces. The gentlemen acknowledged the change most gratefully. They felt that it is indeed the mother's heart that gives the hope and patience needed to endure and save the naughty children of the world.

From this first prison, these plans of helping the female prisoners, by Christian teaching and by employment, and by all kinds of sisterly sympathy and succor, spread throughout England and throughout Christendom.

Ladies of rank throughout Europe, queens, princesses, the Empress of Russia, and good women in every town which possessed a prison, sought to learn the methods which had so transformed the prison of Newgate in London. Associations of ladies were formed everywhere to work these plans out, and much good was done.

What was the secret by which so much effective power was called into action, and the promise of Elizabeth Fry's youth was so abundantly fulfilled, that she should be "eyes to the blind, a tongue to the dumb, and feet to the lame"?

It was the yearning, motherly pity in a woman's heart for her lost sisters, fed by communion with the infinite pity in the heart of the Divine Saviour who came to seek and to save the lost.

It was the undying hope implanted in a woman's heart for those of whom all despaired, and who despaired of themselves.

These poor prisoners were cast out as the refuse of the world. They had deserved and accepted the position. They became refuse indeed, poisoning the air they breathed.

And suddenly, into the depths of their degradation, came down one of the purest and noblest of women, majestic with matronly beauty. . . . She came among them and spoke to them as children of the Heavenly Father, lost and sinful, indeed, but still His children, children He was yearning to welcome back to His heart.

No one had expected them to be anything but wild beasts, and wild beasts they became. She expected them to become good women, and they began once more to be human.

Her winsome and convincing testimony before a committee of the House of Commons and the House of Lords paved the way for the improvement of the prison system throughout the empire.

And through all these public works of Elizabeth Fry was ever flowing a quiet, fresh stream of homelife, overflowing in ceaseless little acts of lovingkindness to all around her. . . .

She was most dearly cherished and honored by all her numerous kindred, husband, children, grandchildren, brothers, sisters, and nieces. In sickness, no one could nurse as she could. She stooped to the humblest services. Her very presence was calming; her soft hand, her exquisite reading, her 'delicious company,' her wonderful power of hoping, cheered and sustained as none else could.

Finally flesh and heart failed, but . . . her spirit, her real being, the love which was her very self, remained the same.

"What should I be without Him?" she said. "Even in sleep, I think the heart is ever lifted up. It is, if I may say it, living in constant communion with Christ. The confidence has never left me that all would be well, if not in time, in eternity. I never lose the feeling of this. I am always on the Rock."

At six o'clock on the morning of one Sunday in October, 1845, she said to the faithful servant who waited on her, "Mary, dear Mary, I am very ill." And then, "Pray for me. It is a strife; but I am safe." After a little while, one of her daughters being there . . . she said, "Oh, my dear Lord! help and keep Thy servant."

Her daughter read the words of the ancient Holy Scriptures: "I the Lord God will hold thy right hand, saying unto thee, Fear not, thou worm Jacob, and ye men of Israel; I will help thee, saith the Lord, and thy Redeemer, the Holy One of Israel."

One bright glance of intelligence and recognition passed over her face as the dear familiar voice uttered the familiar words. It was the last.[1]

ॐ   ॐ   ॐ

Chapter 9

Helper in Word and Deed

"To you I call, O Lord my Rock . . .
Hear my cry for mercy as I call to you for help,
as I lift up my hands toward your Most Holy Place."
(Psalm 28:1-2)

This Psalm was probably written during the time when David was persecuted by Absolom. As David calls out to Jehovah for help, he lifts his hands toward the Most Holy Place. This has reference to the Holy of Holies in the tabernacle, which housed the ark of the covenant. The mercy seat was the lid of the ark:

> Within the ark itself (or in front of it) were Aaron's rod, a pot of manna, and the two tables of the Law. The symbolism of the mercy seat surmounting the tables of the Law is representative of the covering of law by mercy. Thus it speaks of Christ and His perfect atonement that met the demands of the Law, making possible divine mercy. The mercy seat is a type of Christ. Once a year the high priest came with blood to make atonement for his sins and the sins of the people. At the mercy seat God met and communed with those who came through blood. All believers now have access to the mercy seat through Christ, their high priest.[2]

I often think about the Israelites and their curiosity about the Holy of Holies. They must have craved just a glimpse of that Holy place. They must have longed to enter and experience that closeness to the Almighty. And then, at that climatic moment when Jesus "gave up his spirit" (Matthew 27:50), the veil to the Holy of Holies was ripped apart from top to bottom. This dramatically and visually symbolized God saying, "Now you can come! In the New Covenant you can have that intimacy you longed for under the Old Covenant. There is no more wall of separation. The Law has been covered with mercy."

Mercy, according to the dictionary, is "kind and compassionate treatment of an offender, enemy, prisoner, or other person under one's power."[3]

It is no wonder that when David was oppressed he lifted his hands toward the Holy Place, pleading for God's mercy. It is no wonder that the writer of Hebrews used this same Old Testament imagery when explaining the priesthood of Jesus to Jewish believers.

> Therefore, since we have a great high priest who has gone through the heavens, Jesus the Son of God, let us hold firmly to the faith we profess. For we do not have a high priest who is unable to sympathize with our weaknesses, but we have one who has been tempted in every way, just as we are—yet was without sin. Let us then approach the throne of grace with confidence, so that we may receive mercy and find grace to help us in our time of need. (Hebrews 4:14–16)

Because Christ kept the demands of the law on our behalf, and made atonement for our sins, we do not receive what we deserve—the punishment for our sins. Mercy flows from the mercy seat!

Throughout the book of Hebrews the writer explains the mercy of God in Christ Jesus. Then in the conclusion of his letter he exhorts the people, on the basis of the mercy they have received from God, to be merciful. And he puts definition to mercy by giving them examples of what mercy will look like, ". . . keep on loving each other as brothers. Do not forget to entertain strangers, for by so doing some people have entertained angels without knowing it. Remember those in prison as if you were their fellow prisoners, and those who are mistreated as if you yourselves were suffering" (Hebrews 13:1–3). Then he reminds them of their power to be merciful: "God has said, 'Never will I leave you; never will I forsake you.' So we say with confidence,

'The Lord is my helper; I will not be afraid. What can man do to me?' " (Hebrews 13:5–6).

Receiving mercy, not getting all of the punishment we deserve, is a transferring and transforming reality in the life of a Christian. God's mercy *transfers* us from the kingdom of darkness into the Kingdom of light. His mercy *transforms* us from self-centered people to merciful people. Our desire to be merciful emanates from having received mercy. Our power to show mercy comes from the fact that He is with us, He is our helper, He will never leave us. Deeds of charity not done with this motive and power are not Biblical mercy. They are simply humanitarian efforts and, as Isaiah said, "all our righteous acts are like filthy rags" (Isaiah 64:6).

Of course being merciful is a characteristic of every believer, but woman's helper design inclines us to extend mercy in very practical ways.

A BIBLICAL MODEL

Between two episodes of Jesus dealing with large crowds of people, Luke inserts an incident of Jesus helping a woman.

> Jesus left the synagogue and went to the home of Simon. Now Simon's mother-in-law was suffering from a high fever, and they asked Jesus to help her. So he bent over her and rebuked the fever, and it left her. She got up at once and began to wait on them. (Luke 4:38–39)

This is a "potent portion" of Scripture. This is one of those "good things come in small packages" happenings.

Jesus touched her. Her spontaneous reflex was to do what she knew how to do. This is the bent of women. Peter's mother-in-law was not the least inclined to write a position paper on the theology of healing. She was inclined to serve. But there is something else tucked in that event that should not be missed. She reflected the touch of Jesus not just by serving Him. She served *them*. Actually she served *Him* by serving *them*.

God's sovereign love is the fountain of His mercy. As that mercy flows into the life of a believer, it flows out to touch those who need mercy. Peter's mother-in-law was empowered by the touch of Jesus to get up from her sick bed and serve others. Her skills and her scope were limited, but she did what she knew how to do where she was. She extended that merciful touch to those around her. This is the beauty of mercy. It is most extraordinary when it is done in the ordinariness of life.

When a woman yields to her creational design, the marvelous results resonate in every part and season of her life. For many women, these results are first evident in the home. Then, as children grow and leave, there is time for the helper attribute to be "poured forth on a larger world, of the orphans, the sick, the suffering, and the oppressed."[4]

WORD AND DEED

The ministry of the Church is to include word and deed:

> For I will not presume to speak of anything except what Christ has accomplished through me, resulting in the obedience of the Gentiles by word and deed. (Romans 15:18, NAS)

Paul's prayer for the church of the Thessalonians was that God would "strengthen you in every good deed and word" (II Thessalonians 2:17).

The Proverbs 31 woman harmonizes word and deed: "She opens her arms to the poor and extends her hands to the needy" (verse 20). "She speaks with wisdom, and faithful instruction in on her tongue" (verse 26).

A local church will most effectively harmonize word and deed when men and women partner in crafting and implementing the church's vision of ministry. Combining the rational strengths of men and the relational strengths of women will give this vision completeness. It will be both cerebral and emotional. The cerebral will give it doctrinal depth and the emotional will give it energy. Either without the other is incomplete and ineffective. Of course this is not to imply that women bring no intellectual proficiency, or that men bring no affective vitality, to the process. It does mean that completeness and balance are achieved when male and female strengths coalesce.

Men and women must partner to help the victims, the fatherless, the needy, and the afflicted within the Church (see chapter 4), and to extend the ministry of mercy to those outside the Church. Throughout history women's involvement in mercy ministries has been assumed. Before we lost our identity as helpers, women just naturally gravitated to ministries of mercy.

We come to the great organization of charity, the Christian Church, to that great army of succor which has never ceased, since the days when Mary broke the alabaster box on the feet of Christ, and Dorcas made her coats and garments for the poor in Syrian Lydda, and Lydia, the first European Christian, opened her house to the persecuted apostle, to shed the glow of motherly and sisterly loving-kindness through every age, and every part of Christendom, on battle-fields, in hospitals, in prisons, among the outcast, the helpless, the wronged, the sinful, and the lost.

For the whole Church is as a Bride, helpmeet of the mighty Healer and Saviour of the lost world.

The whole Church, in her ideal, is as the heavenly Mother, free and majestic and tender, to gather and succor and save. The whole Christian Church is this in the divine purpose, and has been this in scattered, imperfect human fulfillment through saintly men and women, from age to age, from land to land, never, in any one age or country in which she has existed, having failed to exhibit something of the divine likeness of love.

The women of this army of charity differ in their mode of working, in the objects of their succor, in individual character. But all have this one characteristic. They are stirred by a passion of pity for this suffering, sinful world, inspired by love to the Saviour of the world, sustained by continual communion with Him through prayer.

They are of all ages and of all social classes. Girls of sixteen, moved with this love to God and to His suffering creatures, give the strength and beauty of their youth to cheer the sick and aged. Aged women find the blessed work as heart satisfying in age as in youth.[5]

When women execute their helper design, they are the heartbeat of the Church.

AND THE BEAT GOES ON

Bert Schaffnit is a part of that "great army of succor which has never ceased." Bert's compassion for the elderly prompted her to begin regular visitation to the Bowes Retirement Home in Elgin, Illinois. But her dream to take the love of Jesus to the residents was too big to keep to herself. She involved members of her church, Westminster Presbyterian, by organizing families to conduct a variety of monthly programs including hymn-singing, a brief message from the Word, crafts, musical programs, and refreshments. Even the children are learning at an early age the joy that comes in serving others. Bert's commitment to mercy as a mission in life has enabled her to care enough to enrich the lives of the residents of Bowes Retirement Home and to expand the ministry of mercy in her church.

The women from the Colfax Center Presbyterian Church in Holland, Iowa, have had such a positive presence in their community that they were awarded the 1991 Governor's Award for outstanding volunteer service in the state of Iowa. Their involvement in the "Adopt-A-Family" program won them this recognition. Through this program they helped a low income family by providing help with food and clothing and giving gifts on birthdays and holidays. They also regularly visit three nursing homes in the community, where they provide programs and take cookies and lap robes to the residents.

Lois Coleman became a Christian in 1970 and hasn't slowed down since in her pursuit of serving her Savior. Her focus for the past fifteen years has been on rescuing children from the cycle of inner-city poverty by bringing young girls into her home to raise them with stability, discipline, love, and especially the redeeming love of Jesus Christ. For years she dreamed of a bigger house so she could take in more girls. With the help of churches and other caring individuals in Birmingham, Alabama, her dream has become a reality. Grace House will accommodate up to ten residents who are willing to be molded and influenced by a wholesome and Christian lifestyle as they live with "Mama Lois."

The Cookie Patrol is a creative way to take cleansing mercy to the public square to encourage men addicted to pornography to get help.

> The Cookie Patrol is a group of concerned women who give men entering a pornography outlet a brochure offering counseling for sex addiction. A free cookie, along with the brochure, is also offered to the men in a spirit of love and concern. The Cookie Patrol has been used most successfully in Kansas City. The three-woman patrol covers a particular store during the store's operating hours, rotating in two-hour shifts. . . . In some cities, participating parents have allowed their children to also pass out the cookies and brochures. . . . The volunteers may be nervous, at first, but the patrons of the pornography store are far more embarrassed when confronting the women of the community. . . . Experience in Kansas City shows a dramatic increase in the number of calls to the sex addiction support group mentioned in the brochure. . . . Many men do an about-face and do not patronize the pornography outlet. Some men request prayers or counsel.[6]

Audrey Stallings, from Deland, Florida, heard someone speak about disaster relief. God pricked her heart. She gathered information and attended seminars to become certified in disaster response. When hurricane Andrew hit south Florida, Audrey was ready. She mobilized women from other churches; sorted and organized food donations; issued vouchers for food, clothing, and shelter to disaster and pre-disaster homeless. Audrey is still ready and willing to go whenever and wherever she is needed. When asked what drives her, Audrey replies, "My prayer is that the Lord will use me to reach out and comfort someone."

After hearing a Christian doctor speak of his work with inner city neighborhoods in Wilmington, Delaware, women in several churches responded by collecting items for "comfort kits" which the doctor distributes to the homeless. They contain trial-size items for personal hygiene and tube socks (one size fits all!).

Foothills Presbyterian Church in San Bernardino, California, has less than a hundred members, but they are rich in mercy. Helping others is no small task for the women in this church, since most of them have to work outside the home to help support their families. The church is located in a changing community where poverty, violence, prostitution, drugs, and gangs are commonplace. The food pantry for the poor and homeless, one of the centerpiece ministries of the church, is successful at involving practically every member of the church, including the children. The women's ministry reaches out to Cambodian mothers and their children, providing a neighborhood children's ministry called "Covenant Kids Club," and a weekly Bible study for women. They minister to mentally retarded adults at a nearby group home. Recently when a woman was abandoned by her husband, hungry, pregnant, and about to lose her apartment, the church came to her rescue. They provided food, financial help with the rent, and the love and acceptance that comes when Jesus is shared with those in need. Several times the elders and deacons had to intervene in tense confrontations with the husband. The women from the church shared in the woman's struggles, attended her Lamaze classes, and were there when her child was born. They went with her to court hearings, and when she found a job the women provided childcare for her. And remember, these are women who sometimes have to go to the church's food pantry to feed their own families.

These women understand what James meant when he said, "What good is it, my brothers, if a man claims to have faith but has no deeds? Can such faith save him? Suppose a brother or sister is without clothes and daily food. If one of you says to him, 'Go, I wish you well; keep warm and well fed,' but does nothing about his physical needs, what good is it?" (James 2:13–17).

These women possess that ". . . wisdom that comes from heaven . . . full of mercy and good fruit . . ." (James 3:17).

POURING OUT MERCY

We are the "vessels of His mercy" (Romans 9:23, NAS). It is absolutely wild that God would put this treasure, His mercy, in such unlikely containers. "But we have this treasure in jars of clay to show that this all-surpassing power is from God and not from us. We are hard pressed on every side, but not crushed; perplexed, but not in despair, persecuted, but not abandoned; struck down, but not destroyed" (II Corinthians 4:7–8).

This is spiritually intoxicating! It is exhilarating to realize that this treasure is in me and that the more I pour it out, the more there will be to pour out. Christian women have no reason to be confused about our identity or our calling. There is a world out there that needs us. There is a Helper in our hearts to empower us. Jesus promised this empowerment when He said, "I will ask the Father, and He will give you another Helper, that He may be with you forever; that is the Spirit of truth, whom the world cannot receive, because it does not behold Him or know Him, but you know Him because he abides with you and will be in you" (John 14:16–17).

Don't deprive the part of the world where God has placed you of the treasure in your vessel.

VALETTA STEEL

 The opening stories in the preceding chapters have been from the pages of history. There is something comfortable about the past. I am challenged and inspired, but I can rationalize that such obedience just does not work today. I know better, but I have to make myself admit that obedience to God's Word is not optional, regardless of when or where I live. To help us bridge from the pages of history to the pages of our lives, I have chosen to tell of a contemporary woman in this last story.

Valetta Steel has walked through the valley of the shadow of death for forty years, yet she has walked this path in obedience to Biblical truth.

Valetta was only eighteen when she married Henry Steel in 1950. A year later, while still a student, Henry began his first pastorate in a small country church in Sherwood, Michigan. Their first child, Danny, was born in 1952. Two years later he was diagnosed with leukemia. Their second son, Leon, was just a year old at the time. Danny died shortly after his second birthday.

Their third child, Lorna, was born in 1956. In 1959 Henry and Valetta responded to God's call to missions even though Henry had been diagnosed a Hodgkins patient and told he had only a few years to live. He became Northwest Regional Director, then U.S. Director, of homeland ministries for OMS. This meant a move to Los Angeles. In 1963 Henry died, and Valetta again walked through the valley of the shadow of death.

The thirty-year-old widow was left with the care of two small children and the opportunity to work part-time in the mission office. In 1966 she moved to Indiana when OMS relocated the national headquarters. Nine years after her husband died, Lorna and Leon, and Leon's college friend Don, left home one night to go bowling. Half an hour later a police officer stood at Valetta's door. Valetta tells about this in her book *Thrice Through The Valley:*

"There has been an accident. I'm sorry to have to tell you that your children and their friend have just been killed."

Suddenly I felt as if I had been pushed over a high cliff into a wild seething sea unable to swim. My mind was creating images: Leon and Lorna in their final moment, as the car spun out of control, and then the crunch of metal against their soft flesh. It was too much. The accident which had taken their lives would now surely take mine as well.

But at that very moment, I felt myself in the strong embrace of the Spirit of God. I was being lifted upward, above the cold winter trees, sweetly, securely, into the warm presence of my Father. With a calm, which I instinctively knew had its source from beyond my own being, I heard myself saying, "Officer, I know where they are. They are with God."[1]

The walk through this valley stripped Valetta of her remaining family. But the journey was filled with the dew of God's touch in a growing ministry.

In 1983 Valetta went to Taiwan to work in youth evangelism. One night in 1990, following a dinner with guests in her home, she was alone. A Taiwanese man, addicted to pornography, entered her house, attempted to smother her, and raped her. That night Valetta walked through the valley of a different kind of death. She experienced deep emotional trauma and questions as to where God was that night. But through the Word and the ministry of loving, godly friends, she realized that though God had temporarily lifted the umbrella of protection from her as He did to Job, He would be glorified through it, in answer to prayer.

The rapist was captured and the trial date was set. Eleven other women came forward and pressed charges against him. His past revealed theft, murder and rape. Knowing this, and because of her knowledge that she was a forgiven sinner, Valetta asked the Taiwanese counselor to go to the prison with her to share the Gospel with the condemned man and so she could tell him that she had forgiven him. She left a New Testament and a Bible correspondence course with him.

Before the trial, the man's parents, sister, and son came to see Valetta. They asked her to drop the charges. She explained that she had forgiven him, but that he must suffer the consequences of his sin. She shared the Gospel with them. His sister was very responsive. Also, Valetta's book was shared with the judges and scores of the city's police force. So this violation of her body was used for the salvation of others. God was glorified through her pain.

When asked how she keeps walking through such deep valleys, Valetta responds, "I know God loves me. How do I know? I look at the cross. I also know from studying the missionary, Paul, that suffering was a part of the growth of the early Christians. God would not allow it unless its end results would be positive."

When asked how she could forgive those who caused her such pain, she responds, "I know that apart from grace, I am capable of any offense. I have been forgiven, so I forgive. God's presence, His grace, His Word, as well as the prayers of His people, have sustained me. There are times of uncertainty, but God's Word, showing His love and transcendent purposes, is the foundation of life, and I know that He does not make mistakes."[2]

I must admit that I cannot comprehend the life-journey Valetta has been called to walk. There is just no place in my brain to file that kind and that amount of pain, and I don't need to try. Valetta is the first to tell you that the point of this story is not her pain but God's transcendent love and joy. My response to her story should not be to focus on Valetta's walk, but on the One Who walks with her. The love that is great enough to overwhelm and sustain her is also available to me. The Word that guides her is the same Word that I am to meditate upon and respond to in obedience. And the prayers of God's people that enabled her to minister to others through her suffering are my resource, too. God will supply that living spiritual energy I need to walk the path that demonstrates His glory in my life. But every drop of bitterness, guilt, anger, and so forth. deprives me of a drop of grace and of a redemptive witness of God's goodness. So I must remain empty of self and full of praise for His unsearchable wisdom.

a.   a.   a.

Chapter 10

HELP AND HOPE

"Blessed is he whose help is the God of Jacob,
whose hope is in the Lord his God . . ."
(Psalm 146:5)

We live in a culture void of hope. Woman's helper design uniquely qualifies us to enter this vacuum and to give help by proclaiming the " . . . Hope of Israel, its Savior in times of distress" (Jeremiah 14:8).

In Psalm 146, the words help (*ezer*) and hope are linked together. This is significant. Help apart from hope is superficial and temporary. It is merely a stopgap measure that is a substitute for the real thing. Yet this is what our culture offers. The Church is often as guilty as the culture in giving help without giving hope. We must not fall into the trap of such shallowness.

To understand the connection between hope and help, let's probe Psalm 146.

PSALM 146

The Psalter closes with five Hallelujah Psalms. The word hallelujah comes from the two Hebrew words hallelu (to praise) and yah (from Yahweh). Psalm 146 is a hallelujah to God, the one true Helper.

The Psalmist begins with healthy self-talk as he exhorts himself to a life of praise:

> Praise the Lord.
> Praise the Lord, O my soul.

> I will praise the Lord all my life;
>> I will sing praise to my God as long as I live.

Then he warns of the absolute futility of looking to any other for help:

> Do not put your trust in princes,
>> in mortal men, who cannot save.
> When their spirit departs, they return to the ground;
>> on that very day their plans come to nothing.

Next he catalogs reasons for putting our hope in Jehovah:

> Blessed is he whose help is the God of Jacob,
>> whose hope is in the Lord his God,
> the Maker of heaven and earth,
>> the sea, and everything in them—
>> the Lord, who remains faithful forever.
> He upholds the cause of the oppressed
>> and gives food to the hungry.
> The Lord sets prisoners free,
>> the Lord gives sight to the blind,
> The Lord lifts up those who are bowed down.
>> the Lord loves the righteous.
> The Lord watches over the alien
>> and sustains the fatherless and the widow,
>> but he frustrates the ways of the wicked.

And he concludes with a shout of celebration:

> The Lord reigns forever,
>> your God, O Zion, for all generations.

> Praise the Lord.

The word hope in this Psalm is the Hebrew masculine noun (*seber*) "found only in Psalms 119:116 and 146:5, where both times it refers to God and His Word as the hope of the Psalmist. It looks abroad to that life and deliverance which alone has power to make a person safe (Ps. 119) and happy (Ps. 146)."[3]

So the object of hope is the Sovereign God. The source and sustenance of hope is His Word. And this hope reverberates into a life of safety and happiness not in circumstances, but in the covenant relationship of love with the Object of hope.

The woman who can give authentic help is the one who has come to a place of hopelessness in self that drives her to God's Word where she finds her "help is the God of Jacob," and her "hope is in the Lord." She is qualified to help others because she has an eternal relationship with the Lord and she is saturated with His Word. She points them to the only viable Object of hope by directing them to the only veritable Source of hope. This is authentic help. It does not enable women to luxuriate in the "Slough of Despond," but helps them to find the steps of truth that lead out of the mire.

THE SLOUGH OF DESPOND

In Bunyan's glorious allegory *Pilgrim's Progress,* he tells the story of Christian's journey from the City of Destruction to the Celestial City. Toward the beginning of the journey, Christian falls into the Slough of Despond. "Though he struggled with all his strength and skill, he could not get out. . . . Then I saw a man come to him whose name was Help, and he asked him, 'What are you doing out there?'"

After Christian explains that he fell in, Help asks "But why did you not look for the steps?" When Christian replies that fear took possession of his mind, Help says, "Give me your hand," and he pulls him out.

Then the narrator of the story goes to Help and asks why a fence had not been put around the miry slough so that travelers would not fall in, to which Help responds:

> This miry slough is such a place that cannot be mended. It is the low ground where the scum and filth of a guilty conscience, caused by conviction of sin, continually gather, and for this reason it is called the Slough of Despond. As sinners are awakened by the Holy Spirit and see their vile condition, there arise in their souls many doubts and fears and many discouraging apprehensions, all of which merge and settle in this place. . . . It is not the pleasure of the King that this

place should remain so foul. His laborers, by the direction of His surveyors, have been employed . . . to improve this swamp, and it has swallowed up at least twenty thousand carloads of solid truth, and tons and tons of wholesome instructions, which have been brought at all seasons from every part of the kingdom—and those who know say that the best materials have been brought to make good ground of this place . . . some good and substantial steps have been placed through this slough by order of the Lord of salvation, but at times this marsh spews out a lot of filth, and in times of changing weather the steps are hardly seen. . . . Nevertheless, the steps are there.[4]

It is not the pleasure of our King that we enable women to stay in the slough. It is His pleasure that we give them solid truth and wholesome instruction which provide substantial steps out of the mire. It is His pleasure that we give them Biblical hope.

HANDLES ON HOPE

The steps out of the slough are not a one-two-three formula. These steps of hope are Biblical truth applied to all of life. But Psalm 146 gives three core truths that put handles on hope. Holding on to these handles will help us to locate and follow the steps even when the "marsh spews out a lot of filth, and in times of changing weather the steps are hardly seen."

Handle #1: Psalm 146 Is a Song of Praise

Praise and hope are inseparable. They feed on each other. As we praise God for His character and promises, hope increases. As hope expands, our praise intensifies. Praise is the opposite of pride and the essence of humility because it gives glory to God. Biblical hope is also the antithesis of pride because this is not a hope in self. It rests on the character and promises of God as revealed in His Word.

This does not mean that we ignore pain. But it does mean that we acknowledge God's sovereignty and His love, regardless of circumstances, because our hope is not on what is transitory but on Who is eternal.

The underpinning of this praise and hope is the phenomenal truth that "The Lord reigns forever, your God, O Zion, for all generations" (verse 10).

Handle #2: Psalm 146 Is a Celebration of a Relationship

It is significant that the Psalmist uses two names to refer to God.

The name God is the Hebrew word Elohim. This name expresses the greatness, glory, creative and governing power, excellence, omnipotence and sovereignty of God.

The name Lord is the Hebrew word Jehovah, or Yahweh. This is the proper name of the God of Israel, and it reveals Him as self-existent and unchangeable. This personal name shows that He is the God of covenant faithfulness who has entered into a personal relationship of love with His people. This gives authentic hope because it means that God has dealt with our sin and reconciled us to Himself.

So in this Psalm we see two aspects of God that are essential if we are to place our hope in Him to give the help we need. First, He is absolutely sovereign. Second, He loves us so much that He has entered into a personal relationship with us. Sovereignty without love would be terrifying. Love without sovereignty would be little more than a warm fuzzy. Combined, they provide hope for the helpless.

The person whose help is in the God of Jacob, whose hope is in the Lord his God, is blessed because he has been reconciled to the Lord God.

Handle #3: Psalm 146 Is a Call to the Ministry of Reconciliation

The Psalmist is very deliberate in listing the results of our reconciled relationship with God. God does not enter into this relationship and then back off and leave us to live life removed from His care and concern. Reconciliation is relational. He upholds the cause of the oppressed, gives food to the hungry, sets prisoners free, gives sight to the blind, lifts up those who are bowed down, loves the righteous, watches over the alien, sustains the fatherless and the widow, and frustrates the ways of the wicked.

Perhaps the Psalmist takes such care to show us how God demonstrates this reconciling hope because our relationship with Him should compel us to take up the ministry of reconciliation.

> For Christ's love compels us, because we are convinced that one died for all. . . . And he died for all, that those who live should no longer live for themselves but for him who died for them and was raised again. . . . *All this is from God, who reconciled us to himself through Christ and gave us the ministry of reconciliation.* . . . We are therefore Christ's ambassadors, as though God were making his appeal through us. (II Corinthians 5:14-20, emphasis mine)

Reconciliation—a relationship with God—is our hope. And we are entrusted with this ministry. Woman's creational design is so suited for this task.

RECONCILIATION IS RELATIONAL

Reconciliation implies that there has been alienation. To reconcile is to re-establish the relationship. ". . . when we were God's enemies, we were reconciled to him through the death of his Son" (Romans 5:10). But reconciliation is not just past tense. The passage goes on to say, "how much more, having been reconciled, shall we be saved through his life!" We live in the ongoing reality of reconciliation because of the continuing, living presence of Jesus in our lives! This is true in our vertical relationship with the Lord, but it is also true in our horizontal relationships with one another. There is something so deep and powerful about a reconciled relationship. There is a dimension that defies description.

I saw it illustrated several years ago, and it was as if God carved it on my brain and said, "Do not forget this picture." I was participating in a training seminar for Sunday School teachers. During the break I met Dotty and her son Ben. He was about thirty years old. As we talked, Ben tousled his mother's hair and said, "I'm the one who gave her these gray hairs." They both laughed and then began to tell me the story of his rebellious years. "At one point," Dotty said, "I had to tell him that he either must live by the rules or leave home. He left. There were years of alienation. Then he returned to the Lord and now teaches teenagers in our church." So far the story is not so unusual. Many rebellious teens have left and returned. But what Dotty said next was indelibly inscribed on my memory. "We were so alienated during those years. But now there is a unique bond between us. We can be in different parts of the room and will know what the other is thinking and how the other is reacting to something. There is a remarkable quality to our relationship." I could see it in the way this mother and son looked at each other. I was overwhelmingly aware that this mother had bled love for her son during those times when they were severed, but that their reconciled relationship overpowered those memories.

That picture has come back to me time and again when a wall of separation is erected in a relationship. That memory has given me hope. And I have come to understand experientially the wonder and joy of a reconciled relationship. I have also come to understand that the alienation that necessitates reconciliation is terribly painful. That shouldn't surprise us. When we turned our backs on God, it caused Him great pain. He longed for us to come back. Sacrificing His Son so that we could be reconciled caused a pain beyond our comprehension. I know, too, that just as we must repent of our sin and receive God's forgiveness in order for reconciliation with Him to happen, there must be both repentance and forgiveness on the human level before a relationship is re-established to this dimension. And so often only one person is willing to do the hard and painful work of restoration.

The reconciled relationship between Dotty and her son is beautiful and powerful. But it is just a glimpse of our relationship with our Heavenly Father. Reconciliation is the difference between a hopeful life and a hopeless life. It is the reality we have to share with the world, and the impetus to do the hard work necessary to take up the ministry of reconciliation. And woman's helper design equips us to do this hard work. A woman with a helper heart is willing to "bleed love" as long as necessary to reach her world for Jesus.

A BIBLICAL MODEL

Mary of Bethany had hope. But she knew the pain that had to precede the reality of reconciliation. So six days before the Passover, when Jesus would be crucified, "Mary took about a pint of pure nard, an expensive perfume; she poured it on Jesus's feet and wiped his feet with her hair. And the house was filled with the fragrance of the perfume" (John 12:3).

This is really amazing. The disciples were repeatedly baffled when Jesus spoke of His impending death, but Mary seems to have understood what eluded them. Perhaps when she sat at His feet, she really listened. She apparently knew that Jesus must endure the cross before He would wear the crown. The disciples criticized her for being wasteful, but Jesus came to her defense and said, "She has done a beautiful thing to me. . . . When she poured this perfume on my body, she did it to prepare me for burial. I tell you the truth, wherever this Gospel is preached throughout the world, what she has done will also be told, in memory of her" (Matthew 26:10-13).

What a memorial! And we do remember. Whenever I read this story I can almost smell the fragrance of the perfume, and I can smell the fragrance of her hope. Now hold that thought about fragrance and fast forward to Paul's letter to the Corinthians where he says:

> But thanks be to God, who always leads us in triumphal procession in Christ *and through us spreads everywhere the fragrance of the knowledge of him.* For *we are to God the aroma of Christ* among those who are being saved and those who are perishing. To the one we are the smell of death, to the other, *the fragrance of life.* (II Corinthians 2:14-16, emphasis mine)

For years my mother has worn Tea Rose perfume. Often when we are in an elevator, or at a checkout counter, or at church, someone will appear to be looking for something and then say, "I smell roses but I don't see any. Where is that fragrance coming from?" She never enters a room and announces that she smells like roses, but it is amusing to us how often the fragrance permeates a room and someone notices.

I think that is what reconciling hope is like. When we are "wearing" it, it permeates the place where we are.

THE FRAGRANCE OF LIFE

Bunyan gives another breathtaking word picture when he tells about Christian's journey through the River of Death to the gate of the Celestial City. Hopeful had joined him earlier in his journey. Two men approached them as they neared the river.

> At the sight of the river the pilgrims turned pale, and were silent. The two men said, "You must go through, or you will never get to the gate."
>
> "Is there no other way?" they asked.
>
> "Yes," said the men, "but since the foundation of the world only two, Enoch and Elijah, have been permitted to go that way, nor shall any others ever be so permitted until Christ comes again."
>
> Then they accepted the inevitable. Entering the water, Christian began to sink. He cried to his good friend Hopeful, "I sink in deep water; the billows go over my head; all His waves go over me."
>
> "Be of good cheer," said Hopeful, "I feel the bottom, and it is good."[5]

I have often said that I am thankful for those times when all props were knocked out from under me, not because I enjoy the fear, confusion, and pain, but because those are the times when "I feel the bottom, and it is good." Those are the times when I know most assuredly that "God is our refuge and strength, an ever present help in trouble. Therefore we will not fear, though the earth give way and the mountains fall into the heart of the sea, though its waters roar and foam and the mountains quake with their surging" (Psalm 46:1–3).

Hope shows that there is a way out . . . that the bottom is there and it is good. Hope is not nebulous. A woman who has hope can dispense hope to a needy world in tangible, visible ways. When we do this, we are a "fragrance of life" in our culture.

We *are* a fragrance of life. We are the perfume bottle. This is *what* we are by virtue of *Whose* we are. We have been reconciled to the King of the universe and His Spirit is inside of us, so we are the aroma of Christ. Some will be enticed by this aroma. Some will be allergic to it. Some will think our perfume stinks. The response of others is not our responsibility. Removing the lid of our perfume bottle so that the fragrance is evident is our responsibility. Removing the lid does not mean that we enter a room, or a relationship, and announce that we are wearing the fragrance of life. It does mean that our presence sends off a fragrance that softly and gently wafts through the space where we are until someone says, "I smell roses."

A distressing thing to me about our perfume is that I smell it in our churches, but I don't smell it in our culture. And if I understand the Maker and Bottler of our perfume, He has commissioned us to wear it in public.

When Jesus authorized us to be fragrance bearers for His Kingdom, he gave us a grand commission. It goes something like this:

> The moral decay around you is overwhelming. There is no hope that you can do anything to make a significant difference, so just withdraw into your holy huddles, enjoy one another's fragrance, and wait until I come back.

Not! And yet often we act as if that is our assignment.

Our King told us in no uncertain terms to go: "All authority in heaven and on earth has been given to me, therefore go and make disciples of all nations, baptizing them in the name of the Father and of the Son and of the Holy Spirit, and surely I will be with you always, to the very end of the age" (Matthew 28:18–20).

So where do we go? It depends on where you are.

What do we do? We show that there is hope by being a fragrance of life, the aroma of Christ.

WOMEN WHO WEAR THE FRAGRANCE OF LIFE

Dr. Carolyn Cain is a fragrance of life in the medical arena. Carolyn is doing her internship in pediatrics. Interns are required to sleep at the hospital when they are on call. In Carolyn's hospital, there is only one call room where interns sleep with their medical student, male or female. As a Christian, this was unacceptable for Carolyn. Carolyn and her husband prayed, then she went to the chief resident. She did not go belligerently. She did not go waving her Bible. She went gently and humbly and simply explained that she was uncomfortable with the arrangement. The subject had never been raised by anyone else. But Carolyn was heard and accommodation was made. A small but important change was made for women in the medical profession because a Christian woman was willing to be a fragrance of life.

Norma Bourne is an aroma of Christ from her wheelchair. Norma has cerebral palsy, and her mother Ruth is her primary caregiver, her constant companion and closest friend. These women are pillars in the First Presbyterian Church in North Port, Florida. Norma has learned to use a computer, and she prepares the church bulletin, the monthly newsletter and the treasurer's reports. Together Norma and Ruth send out, grade, and process Bible courses to English-speaking people in the Caribbean. They are passionate about the pro-life movement, and it is not uncommon to see them picketing in front of a local abortuary. And when the church softball team plays, Norma and Ruth are on the sideline lending their special cheers of encouragement. Norma and Ruth do not let a wheelchair, widowhood, or any other circumstance keep them from wearing their perfume in the place where God has put them.

Pat Newlin wears the fragrance of life into the marketplace. Christ entered Pat's life through someone she worked with. She says that was probably the only way to get her attention, since she was a classic workaholic who labored long and hard to create a world-class public relations agency in New York City. She joined Redeemer Presbyterian Church, and it made a profound change in her life. "I had spent the last ten years in a homosexual relationship. I felt that that was who I was and that was what my identity was. But as I listened to the sermons at church and began to study the Bible, I began to understand the work of the Holy Spirit within me. I felt the healing happening. There is no other way to explain it. I suddenly realized that I was no longer dead. It was profound. It was a healing." The self-described hard-charging New York executive now views her life, work, and relationships from the perspective of glorifying the Lord God, and those around her "smell the roses."

Joyce Horton takes the sweet fragrance into a woman's prison in Mississippi. "One day in my devotions I was smitten with Christ's statement that if I had never visited the jail, I had never visited Him in jail! I didn't make any virtuous commitment, I simply realized that I would be called upon to do that someday and, as distasteful as it sounded, I would have to do it. Soon I was asked to accompany a group on a Sunday afternoon jail visit, assured that I wouldn't have to say a thing—just fill an empty spot. I was confident I would only have to go once. So I went, thinking, 'Thank you, Lord, for the opportunity to get this checked off my list of obedience!' But several months later a long-time friend, the chaplain of Central Mississippi Correctional Facility, the women's penitentiary in my area, asked me if I would teach weekly Bible studies to the new inmates and in one zone of Maximum Security Unit, since these groups could not leave their buildings to attend services at the chapel. I accepted. Bible teaching is my favorite activity, but I could not get a lesson prepared. My minister told me that I was going into Satan's territory and that I was under attack. He prayed for and with me, and immediately everything began to fall into place."

Many women and children have surrounded Joyce with their prayers and support. Women in many churches collect toiletries, Christian reading material, pens and paper, candy, sweaters, crochet yarn, and many other items. Youth groups pack these items in boxes for Joyce to deliver. Children save their Sunday School papers for her to take to the prison. "The women love getting these papers to give to their children on visitation day," says Joyce. Joyce carries hope to hopeless women as she wears the fragrance of life into a prison.

These daughters of Zion dispense authentic hope as they live out their relationship with Jesus Christ in whatever arena He places them. They demonstrate that Christianity is a better way. They override our vain and vacuous culture with validity and valor. They are a fragrance of life.

PIONEER WOMEN

I have only driven through the Western states once, but on that trip I often thought of the brave women who made those first excursions through that beautiful but formidable territory. I imagined them packing their belongings and their children in a covered wagon and setting out on an incredible adventure. There surely were moments when they looked at the vast expanse of land and sky before them and longed to return to the safety of the secure. My imagination peaked as I thought of those pioneer women making the courageous decision to blaze a trail into that enormous expanse. But the 90s woman has an equally exciting opportunity to be on the cutting edge. When we accept the challenge to display our helper design, we will be pioneers blazing a trail through the vast expanse of hopelessness before us.

The Master Designer has fashioned us for the task. When His daughters display His design, I believe our culture will be so captivated by the beauty that culture can be captured for King Jesus.

> How blessed is he who considers the helpless.
> The Lord will deliver him in a day of trouble.

The Lord will protect him and keep him alive,
and he shall be called blessed upon the earth.
(Psalm 41:1–2, NAS)

I will lift up my eyes to the hills—
where does my help come from?
My help comes from the Lord,
the Maker of heaven and earth.
He will not let your foot slip—
he who watches over you will not slumber;
indeed, he who watches over Israel will neither
slumber nor sleep.

The Lord watches over you—
the Lord is your shade at your right hand;
the sun will not harm you by day,
nor the moon by night.

The Lord will keep you from all harm—
He will watch over your life;
the Lord will watch over your coming and going
both now and forevermore. (Psalm 121)

CONCLUSION

Writing this book has been exhilarating, exhausting, and embarrassing.

It has been exhilarating because I was so pregnant with a passion to challenge the church to encourage and equip women to unfurl our helper design before the world that I thought I would explode if this passion was not birthed. It has also been exhilarating because I am not a writer. I can remember breaking out in a cold sweat in high school when my English teacher would tell us to take out pen and paper and write a theme. I had difficulty getting through English composition in college. It is wild that God would use me to write a book! So the experience has been exhilarating because every paragraph represents a time of intense fellowship with the Lord.

Writing this book has been exhausting because writing is laborious. But the long hours and the tedious work are only part of the picture. There has been emotional exhaustion as I remember the faces of the women who have shared their stories of abuse and pain. There has been spiritual exhaustion as fierce spiritual warfare has raged around me as I have written against distortions of truth. But notice I said "raged around me"—part of the exhilaration was the strong realization that the war did not quite touch me as I worked on this book. It was as if there was a protection around me. And then I would get a note from a woman saying that she did not know why, but God had impressed her to pray for me every day! How exhilarating!

You are probably saying, "Exhilarating and exhausting I understand, but why embarrassing?"

Remember, I am not a writer. Some of the embarrassment is probably prideful fear that you will laugh at what I have written.

But most of the embarrassment is because writing this book has been like unzipping my flesh and exposing the deepest crevices in my soul. That is a terribly vulnerable position! So why have I done it? I have asked myself that question many times. Between chapters nine and ten I took a day off and spent it with my grandchildren. That was not the only break I took. Between chapters six and seven Gene and I went to Switzerland for two weeks! But somewhere around chapter eight or nine I was slipping. All the words and thoughts were running together and everything was fuzzy. I had serious questions about why I was exerting so much energy. I was feeling cautious and fearful about tackling such hard issues. Why expose myself to attacks from those who disagree with what I have said? But as Hunter, Mary Kate and I read books, drew pictures, talked, and laughed, and as I rocked and fed baby Daniel, I knew afresh why I had to write this book.

Twenty years from now Hunter, Mary Kate, and Daniel are going to look at me and ask, "Me-mommie, what were you doing in the 1990s when America was going through a cultural war and Biblical truth was being distorted?" I am not about to say, "Oh, I shopped 'till I dropped!" or "Well, I improved my golf game," or "That was dirty work, and I couldn't get involved because I may have broken my acrylic fingernails."

Of course there is nothing wrong with shopping, golf, or acrylic fingernails, but sometimes it seems as if many women have slipped into a comfortable cocoon, and they never emerge. If you talk about the reality of abortion, pornography, abuse, or AIDS, they look at you with their eyes glossed over as if you are talking about something in outer space. They act as if there is no world beyond their cocoon. And yet that is the world their grandchildren are growing up in. I am terrified of the cocoon. I plead with the Lord to never let me slip into such creature comfort that I am no longer an aroma of the knowledge of Christ to a hurting world.

There is another reason I have felt compelled to write this book. I am a privileged woman. The privilege I refer to is that I have a husband who encourages me to be all that God created me to be and to do what God calls me to do. Gene blends strength and humility in a profound way. Perhaps it is this humble strength that produces his conviction that to stifle me would be selfish disobedience to our God. Submission to such godly headship is a privileged position for which I am grateful. Great privilege carries responsibility.

I can't do a lot, but I do not want to be guilty of doing nothing.

I want to be like the women I have told about in this book. These women, and thousands of others like them, are not living in a cocoon. They are real women living in the real world. They are living out the helper design in their homes, neighborhoods, and communities. I want to be counted among their number, and I want you to be counted among their number. The real story is not our individual stories, but the totality of the obedience of the daughters of Zion.

> "Sing, O Daughter of Zion;
> shout aloud, O Israel!
> Be glad and rejoice with all your heart,
> O Daughter of Jerusalem!
> The Lord has taken away your punishment,
> he has turned back your enemy.
> The Lord, the King of Israel, is with you;
> never again will you fear any harm.
> On that day they will say to Jerusalem
> Do not fear, O Zion;
> do not let your hands hang limp,
> The Lord your God is with you,
> he is mighty to save.
> He will take great delight in you,
> he will quiet you with his love,
> he will rejoice over you with singing. . . .
> At that time I will gather you;
> at that time I will bring you home.
> I will give you honor and praise
> among all the peoples of the earth
> when I restore your fortunes
> before your very eyes," says the Lord. (Zephaniah 3:14–20)

Our obedience will cause our Father to rejoice over us with singing, and He will gather us—He will bring us home! We need no other motivation.

THE FINAL WORD

I have leaned so heavily on the out-of-print book *The Women of Christendom* that it seems only right to let the dear daughter of Zion who authored that inspiring work have the last word. It's not only right, it's expedient. She has already expressed so beautifully what I want to say, so it is senseless for me to restate it. And to be perfectly honest, Hunter just called and asked if he and Mary Kate and Daniel could come over and play with Gene and me.

And so the stories I have to tell you now have come to an end.

No cold gravestones are these memorials, but sun-pictures of our beloved ones who are withdrawn from our sight for a time, but whom we hope one day to see. No records are they of the triumphs of a power grown feeble, or of a Creed grown obsolete. They are but leaves from the tree of life which is for the healing of the nations, always life and always healing, whether found in the chilliest zones of Christendom or in the most tangled wildernesses of its tropical luxuriance.

We have gone, have we not? as we intended, into home after home, and have seen how the divine life has entered there, the life of divine love and faith and hope, life in Him who is our life, and made conquests within and around of discord and despair and sin.

We have seen this life of love, adoring and serving, manifested in women of all classes and characters, shining from the quiet depths of homes in blessing on all around, diffusing through the wide world the love which is the light of the home, seeking, saving, serving. . . .

And these, we must always remember, are no exceptional portraits of an exceptional aristocratic caste of inimitable saints. They are specimens of the universal Christian life demanded of us all, lived by not a few; not perfect, indeed, but being perfected; not, indeed, complete in any one; complete only in Him, who is the Head and Life of all, and in His whole Body, which is the Church.

Nor, thank God, are they records of a race and a life passed away.

At this moment I could lead you into home after home around us now, blessed and hallowed by lives as Christ-like and humble and sweet.

I could show you, one after another, maiden and matron, young and aged, poor and princely, going forth into the world to nurse the sick, to raise the fallen, to teach the ignorant, to succor the needy, to save the sinful and the lost. And all alike inspired by the one sacrifice of Jesus, the Son of God; all, in the lowliest services as in the extremist agonies, strengthened by His imperishable "unto me;" all, indeed, not so much consciously following His footsteps, as actually living out the life of Him who "came not to be ministered unto, but to minister, and to give His life a ransom for many," "to seek and save that which was lost;" who gave not the worlds He created, nor even only the life-blood of His human heart for us, but Himself, to redeem us to God.[1]

NOTES

Introduction

1. *Sketches of The Women of Christendom,* by the author of *Chronicles of the Schonberg-Cotta Family,* (New York: Dodd, Mead & Company, n.d.), pp. 1–2, 186–187.

Chapter 1: Distinctiveness

1. All quotes and information in this story are from J. H. Alexander, *Ladies of the Reformation* (England: Gospel Standard Strict Baptist Trust, Ltd., 1978), pp. 119–122.

2. Janette Hassey, *No Time For Silence* (Grand Rapids, MI: Zondervan, 1986), p. 23.

3. *Ibid.,* pp. 23-24.

4. Harvel Kidder, *The Kids' Book of Chess.*

5. James B. Hurley, *Man and Woman in Biblical Perspective,* (Grand Rapids, MI: Zondervan, 1981), p. 209.

6. R. Laird Harris, Gleason L. Archer, Jr., and Bruce K. Waltke, *Theological Wordbook of the Old Testament,* vol 2 (Chicago: Moody Press, 1981), p. 661.

Chapter 2: Distortions

1. *Sketches of The Women of Christendom,* p. 293 passim.

2. From an unpublished paper by Georgia Settle entitled "Feminism: Freedom Without Purpose,"

3. Peter Jones, *The Gnostic Empire Strikes Back* (Phillipsburg, NJ: P & R Publishing, 1992), p. 62–63. [Jones quotes from George Gilder, *Sexual Suicide* (New York: New York Times, 1973) which was revised under the title *Men and Marriage* (Gretna: Pelican, 1986).]

4. *Ibid.* p. 63.

5. Mary A. Kassian, *The Feminist Gospel,* (Wheaton, IL: Crossway, 1992), p. 159.

6. *Ibid.*, p. 225, 239.

7. Settle, "Feminism: Freedom Without Purpose."

8. Ron Rhodes, "The Debate over Feminist Theology," *Christian Research Journal* (Summer 1991).

9. *Ibid.*

10. John Leo, "The Trouble with Feminism," *U.S. News & World Report,* (February 10, 1992).

11. Cal Thomas, Los Angeles Times Syndicate.

12. John Piper and Wayne Grudem, *Recovering Biblical Manhood & Womanhood, A Response to Evangelical Feminism,* edited by (Wheaton, IL: Crossway Books, 1991), p. xiii.

Chapter 3: Defenders of Truth

1. All quotations and information in this story from Eileen Dunkerly, "Women of the Covenant," *Presbyterian Journal* (October 1985). This magazine which was published in Weaverville, NC, is no longer in existence.

2. L. Berkhof, *Systematic Theology,* (Grand Rapids, MI: Eerdmans, 1977), p. 558.

3. *Ibid.,* p. 595.

4. I would not allow myself to read this book until after I had written chapters 3, 4, and 5. I had to be sure that what I said was what the Lord had put on *my* heart. One of my fears about these chapters was the realization that they would probably "rattle some cages." Reading *The Body* relieved that fear—Charles Colson and Ellen Santilli Vaughn have already rattled the cages!

5. Charles Colson with Ellen Santilli Vaughn, *The Body* (Dallas, TX: Word, 1992), p. 32.

6. This topic is addressed more completely in my book *Spiritual Mothering,* (Wheaton, IL: Crossway, 1992).

7. Jane Ferguson is now Jane Niederbrach and is living in Chicago with her husband.

8. Berkhof, p. 558.

Chapter 4: Defenders of Women

1. Dunkerley, "Women of the Covenant," *Presbyterian Journal,* (October, 1985).

2. This subject is addressed more fully in a book I co-wrote with Peggy Hutcheson entitled *Leadership For Women In The Church* (Grand Rapids, MI: Zondervan).

3. This poem is copyrighted, but the name is withheld at the request of the writer.

4. An example of a survey is given in the Leader's Guide for this book which can be ordered by calling: 1-800-283-1357.

Chapter 5: Deliverance

1. George Grant, *Third Time Around, A History of the Pro-Life Movement from the First Century to the Present,* (Brentwood, TN: Wolgemuth & Hyatt, Publishers, Inc., 1991), p. 69–72.

2. Harris, vol 2, p. 716.

3. For a detailed discussion of the relationship between Mary and Elizabeth, I refer you to my book *Spiritual Mothering,* (Wheaton, IL: Crossway, 1992).

4. In *The Body*, Colson and Vaughn explain that:

> the therapeutic gospel . . . works from the outside in to restore self-esteem by enabling us to adjust to our circumstances; carried far enough, it can lead us to feel good about being bad. The gospel, on the other hand, is designed to transform our lives and circumstances; it works from the inside out. Therapy is concerned with changing behavior; the gospel, with changing character. Therapy gives us what we think we need; the gospel gives us what we really need . . . Psychology or psychiatry can play an important role in helping. But behavior science cannot be blended into the gospel, either in counseling or, least of all, in the message preached. (p. 123)

5. Obviously this is cursory look at forgiveness, but since there is a chapter on this topic in *Spiritual Mothering,* I will refer the reader once again to that book.

6. *Jerdone Davis Newsletter,* (March 23, 1993).

Chapter 6: Helper-Defender

1. All quotes and information in this story are from R. Pierce Beaver, *American Protestant Women In World Mission* (Grand Rapids, MI: Eerdmans, 1968), p. 9–19.

2. John Calvin, *Commentaries on The Four Last Books of Moses,* (Grand Rapids, MI: Baker Book House, 1981), p. 298.

3. Charles Colson, *Against The Night,* (Ann Arbor, MI: Servant Publications, 1989), p. 137.

4. Edith Schaeffer, *The Life of Prayer*, (Wheaton, IL: Crossway, 1992), p. 34–35.

5. C. Peter Wagner, *Prayer Shield*, (Ventura, CA: Regal Books, 1992), p. 50.

6. Reprinted from the newsletter of First Presbyterian Church, Columbia, SC.

7. *Sketches*, pp. 184-185.

8. Wagner, p. 50.

Chapter 7: Helper-Supporter

1. *Sketches*, pp. 258–78.

2. William Bradford, *Bradford's History of the Plymouth Settlement, 1608-1650*, translated into modern English by Harold Paget (Portland, OR: American Heritage Ministries, [1909] 1899), p. 21. Cited by Gary DeMar, *America's Christian History: The Untold Story*, (Atlanta, GA: American Vision, Publishers, Inc., 1993), p. 34.

3. Harris, vol. 2, pp. 945–46.

4. James Dobson, *Dr. Dobson Answers Your Questions* (Wheaton, IL: Tyndale House, 1989), pp. 412–14.

Chapter 8: Helper-Protector

1. From a telephone interview with Bill Armes.

2. *Matthew Henry's Commentary on the Whole Bible*, vol. III, (New York: Fleming H. Revell Co., n.d.), p. 673.

3. James Dobson and Gary Bauer, *Children At Risk*, (Dallas: Word, 1990), p. 155.

4. *Ibid.*, p. 156.

5. William Ross Wallace, *The Hand That Rules the World*, Stanza 1, 1819-1881.

6. Kay Coles James with Jacqueline Cobb Fuller, *Never Forget*, (Grand Rapids, MI: Zondervan, 1992), p. 47, 50, 70–71.

7. From an unpublished paper by Dr. Robert S. Rayburn.

8. Dobson and Bauer, p. 261.

Chapter 9: Helper in Word and Deed

1. *Sketches*, pp. 303–17.

2. *Harper Study Bible* Grand Rapids, MI: Zondervan, 1985), notes on Exodus 25.

3. *The American Heritage Dictionary of the English Language*, (Boston: American Heritage Publishing Co., Inc., and Houghton Mifflin Co., 1969).

4. *Sketches*, p. 280.

5. *Ibid.*, pp. 280–81.

6. National Coalition Against Pornography, "What One Woman Can Do," *Take Action Manual of the Enough Is Enough! Campaign*, p. 27. Write to the National Coalition Against Pornography, P.O. Box 888, Fairfax, VA 22030.

Chapter 10: Help and Hope

1. Valetta Steel, *Trice Through the Valley*, (Greenwood, IN: OMS International, 1986), pp. 13–14. This helpful book may be ordered from: Book Room, OMS International, Box A, Greenwood, IN 46142.

2. This story is used by permission. From material written by Valetta's sister-in-law Lela Steel and from a telephone conversation with Valetta.

3. Harris, vol. 2, p. 870.

4. John Bunyan, *Pilgrim's Progress in today's English*, translated into modern English by James H. Thomas, (Chicago: Moody Press, 1964), p. 17-18.

5. *Ibid*, p. 151.

Conclusion

1. *Sketches*, pp. 331–34.

ABOUT THE AUTHOR

Susan Hunt is a pastor's wife. She and her husband Gene have three adult children and three grandchildren. She currently serves as Consultant to "Women in the Church" for the Presbyterian Church in America. She has degrees from the University of South Carolina and Columbia Theological Seminary.

This is Mrs. Hunt's fourth book. Her other books include: *Spiritual Mothering: The Titus 2 Principle of Older Women Mentoring Younger Women,* co-published by Legacy Communications and Crossway Books; *Leadership for Women in the Church,* co-authored with Peggy Hutcheson, and published by Zondervan; and *ABC Bible Verses for Children.*

Susan may be contacted through the Christian Education office of the Presbyterian Church in America:

1852 Century Place, Suite 101
Atlanta, GA 30345
(404) 320-3388

LEGACY COMMUNICATIONS is an explicitly Christian ministry committed to help the Church apply the truths from God's Word to every area of life and demonstrate to the Church and Christian community what the practical implications of this effort are: to develop a Christian and Biblical view towards our culture, specifically, and the world, in general.

Through research, publishing, seminars, audio, and video productions, LEGACY COMMUNICATIONS strives to bring strategic and substantive focus on the grave dilemmas of our day from the perspective of a distinctively forthright Christian worldview. Creating tools that equip the saints for the work of the ministry, filling the gap where commercial enterprises leave off, and forging ahead into previously uncharted realms, is not just what we do—it is what we are.

To receive a free sample of the LEGACY newsletter and information about other books and resources send $1.00 to: Legacy Communications, Post Office Box 680365, Franklin, Tennessee 37068.

A Leader's Guide for *Spiritual Mothering* is available for small group study. To order, call the Christian Education Publications Bookstore at 1-800-283-1357, or order from your local Christian Bookstore.